No Pizza. No Lasagne. No Directions

Sign on the door of a small osteria
in the Santa Croce district of Venice.

POLPO

A VENETIAN COOKBOOK
(OF SORTS)

RUSSELL NORMAN

PHOTOGRAPHY BY JENNY ZARINS

BLOOMSBURY

LONDON · NEW DELHI · NEW YORK · SYDNEY

First published in 2012

Copyright © 2012 by Russell Norman
Photography © 2012 by Jenny Zarins
except photograph on page 301 (bottom right), 304 (bottom), 305 (bottom)
© Russell Norman

Cover illustration by Alcide d'Orbigny (1802–1857). Reproduced by
permission of General Research Division, New York Public Library,
Astor, Lenox and Tilden Foundations.
Map on pages 296–7 © Mary Evans Picture Library

Bloomsbury Publishing Plc, 50 Bedford Square, London WC1B 3DP
Bloomsbury USA, 1385 Broadway, Fifth Floor, New York, NY 10018

www.bloomsbury.com

Bloomsbury is a trademark of Bloomsbury Publishing Plc.
Bloomsbury Publishing, London, Oxford, New York, New Delhi and Sydney

A CIP catalogue record for this book is available from the British Library.
Cataloging-in-Publication Data is available from the Library of Congress.

UK ISBN 978 1 4088 1679 0
US ISBN 978 1 60819 909 9

Design by Praline
Photography by Jenny Zarins
Index by Vicki Robinson

UK: 21
US: 13

Printed in China by C & C Offset Printing Co Ltd. All papers used
by Bloomsbury Publishing are natural, recyclable products made from wood
grown in well-managed forests. The manufacturing processes conform to the
environmental regulations of the country of origin.

OVEN TEMPERATURES

The temperatures in these recipes are for conventional ovens. Fan-assisted oven
temperatures should be lowered by 10°C or even 20°C (1 or 2 Gas marks)
depending on your oven.

ZE MINIME PERMESSE
VENDITA DEL PESCE
SEGUENTI QUALITÁ

	CENT.
A. SARDELLA. SARDON	7
ADA. DENTAL. CORBO	
O. BOSEGHET. SOASO	12
MECIATO. VERZELATA	
PASSARIN. ROMBO	
	25
	5
	3
	3,37

ANTICA ADELAIDE

3728

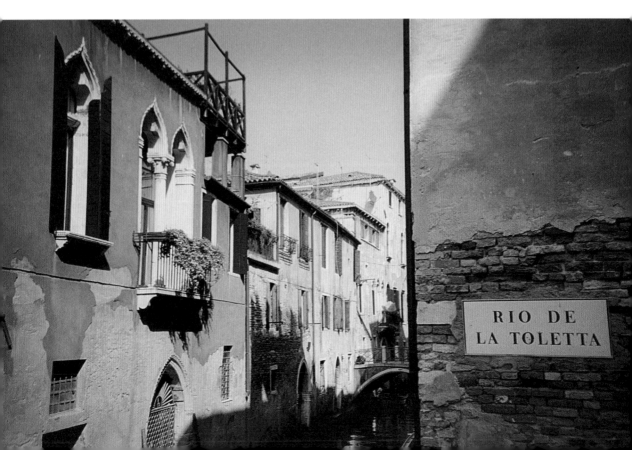

Venice is a city built on water. It is preposterous. If you couldn't see it with your own eyes and touch it with your own fingers, you would think it was some poetic fancy. It really shouldn't be there at all. But it is. And it is beautiful beyond words.

I first visited Venice as a student in the late 1980s. A college friend was spending a summer there with his Italian girlfriend whose mother, a poet, lived in the Giardini district of the city where the Grand Canal widens to join the lagoon. He suggested I travel from France where I was spending my summer to join them for a few days. All the arrangements were made by letter – this was before the era of emails and mobile phones.

I got a cheap ticket on the Orient Express from Paris and had to stand in a corridor for the entire journey. I had half a filled baguette, a bottle of water and a packet of Gitanes. I was happy.

Arriving in Venice by railway is a complete red herring. The train station, Santa Lucia, is austere and modernist, built in the twenties and thirties in a style that would have pleased Mussolini. I really had no idea what to expect from the city, only the vague notion that there would be lots of marble and that there might be a canal or two at some point.

I have a vivid memory of emerging into bright sunlight and searing August heat, walking down the wide steps outside the station, and stopping and staring, eyes on stalks, head spinning. Venice does that to you.

Here in front of me was a city of mind-boggling majesty. Visitors to Florence, Italy's second-most beautiful city, sometimes complain of Stendhal Syndrome – a feeling of being overwhelmed by beauty. I was feeling gobsmacked just standing by the bus stop and I had been here only ten minutes.

I jumped on the Number 1 vaporetto – the waterbus that rides the length of the Grand Canal from Ferrovia to Lido at a steady five kilometres per hour – and tried to take the city in. We passed buildings and structures that seemed familiar and strange at the same time. Rialto Bridge, the fish market, the museums of Ca' Pesaro and Accademia, the church of Santa Maria della Salute, the Doge's Palace, Hotel Danieli... Venice seemed less and less real as we sailed further into the city centre. I started to hallucinate that it was a gigantic film set, impossibly floating on emerald green water.

Then I arrived at Giardini in the Castello district, mercifully free of tourists, even in August, but still within walking distance of St Mark's Square and a single waterbus stop from the beaches of Lido. I spent a week there with my friends and I suppose that's when my affair with Venice started.

In the early years of our courtship, my wife Jules and I travelled to Venice many times. We made the obligatory visits to the appropriate galleries and paid homage to the requisite architecture, but I also became really interested in the food and drink.

Venice's restaurants have an appalling reputation – one that is largely justified, principally because of the shocking food you find in the tourist-trap joints around the hubs of St Mark's Square and Rialto Bridge. These places appeal to the lowest-common-denominator needs of the weary tourist who has been on his feet all morning and has developed a carbohydrate deficiency that can be quelled only by mounds of lasagne, bowls of spaghetti and plates of pizza. Abysmal, and about as authentic as the plastic golden gondolas for sale on Ruga dei Oresi in Rialto.

What interested me were glimpses of tiny wine bars in alleys where locals would stand at the counter, a luminous orange drink in one hand and a small snack in the other. You could tell they were locals because they wore dark clothes or market traders' overalls and shouted at each other in dialect. And they were mostly tourist-free; barely a backpack, map or baseball cap in sight.

Once I had found the courage to enter one of these places, point at the bright orange drink, jab a finger at the pre-made snacks in a glass cabinet on the bar and attempt to work out what the hell was going on, I was hooked. There was no going back. My restaurant radar had kept me away from the horrors of the tourist traps with their leather-bound menus, bottles of Chianti in woven straw baskets and waiters with black waistcoats and terrifying moustaches. And thank goodness. Here was real Venice.

These backstreet bars, known locally as bàcari, served small plates of authentic Venetian titbits, known as cichèti, and were places where locals would meet, drink, eat, argue and gossip. They were like tiny canteens of great humility and simplicity. They provided a public service by offering the city's workers, movers and shakers a place to refuel. They were basic, they lacked vanity and the food on offer was elemental, made up of one or two fresh ingredients; unpretentious and honest. They were Venice's culinary pit-stops. My interest in the galleries and museums, in the art and architecture (for most people, the principal reason to go to Venice in the first place) dwindled to a barely significant distraction. My fascination in these democratic watering holes grew. Oh, and the glowing orange drink? That was a Spritz – a slug of Aperol mixed with local white wine and soda garnished with a lemon slice and an olive.

Subsequent visits to Venice were all about the bàcari. I found myself working for a succession of London restaurant companies and would travel to Venice for holidays and short breaks. My day job in London was all fancy menus and white linen tablecloths, but my leisure and holiday time was spent in Venetian wine bars. I was drawn again and again to their simplicity and honesty. I started collecting ideas and recipes but without really knowing why.

One visit in particular in April 2008, I was eating a warm octopus salad at the bar of Alla Vedova in Cannaregio. I was thinking about the Italian word for octopus, polpo, and musing that it would be a fun name for a restaurant. The penny dropped and I realized that I had the beginnings of an idea. I got incredibly excited by the thought of building a version of a bàcaro in London: Venetian cichèti adapted for metropolitan sensibilities in a relaxed and slightly jaded urban setting. The emphasis would be on simplicity, in terms of menu offer, wine list, design and delivery. Late in 2008, with the restaurant idea firm, recipes stuffed into a scrapbook and a business plan, I resigned as operations director of a fancy corporate restaurant group, got a tattoo of an octopus on my back, and POLPO was born.

The college friend who I stayed with on my first trip to Venice was Richard Beatty. We became best friends and have remained so for more than twenty-five years. He encouraged me to quit my job. He also put his money where his mouth was and backed the project. Oddly, this happened at exactly the same time as the start of the biggest global recession of our lifetime.

Several people questioned our sanity, but Richard and I became fixated on the idea that this was *precisely* the right time to open a casual restaurant serving great value small-plates in a pared-back, noisy setting. I travelled back and forth between London and Venice, obsessing over the tiniest details, photographing paintwork, linen curtains and street signs. I compared the way that different bars made their Spritz and how different places cooked their calf's liver. I collected butcher-paper place mats, wondering how I might source them in England. I scrutinized the tiny wine glasses used in the bàcari and the toothpick-skewered snacks behind the glass cabinets on the counter tops.

Back in London, our search for premises took an interesting turn. We were offered a site on Beak Street in Soho that had a blue plaque announcing that the painter Canaletto once lived and worked there. Canaletto – the most famous Venetian painter of the Baroque era. We smiled at the coincidence but realized that the site was too narrow and turned it down.

After another month of searching, without any luck, I happened to be passing Beak Street and noticed the 'Lease For Sale' sign remained in the window. I called the agent and, sure enough, the site was still available. Was it worth another look?

Richard and I went back and stood in the narrow space, scratching our heads. If only we knew what lay behind the plaster wall. While the agent turned a blind eye, Richard picked up a chair and punched a hole through it. I put my hand into the void and my arm disappeared up to the elbow. There was another 18 inches of width. In a previous refurbishment the tenants must have wanted straight walls, and had plaster-boarded over the alcoves and recesses. (The subsequent strip-out uncovered all sorts of lovely features: fireplaces, 300-year-old timber-framed brick walls, glazed tiles, Victorian steel girders – all hidden for most of the twentieth century.) We made an offer on the spot and, once the legals were agreed, started building a month later.

For the head chef, we were fortunate to find a young chap called Tom Oldroyd who had cooked for a few years at Alastair Little in Soho, an iconic restaurant that Richard and I used to visit frequently. Straight away, Tom and I went to Venice for a short trip. We immersed ourselves in the bàcari and osterie, eating everything and picking dishes apart, making notes and taking photographs. Tom persuaded a few chefs to let him help out in their kitchens and we generally absorbed as much of the culinary energy of the city as we possibly could.

POLPO opened on 30 September 2009, exactly one year after Lehman Brothers filed for bankruptcy protection and kick-started the global economic meltdown. Those friends and family who told us we were mad to open a restaurant in a recession were waiting to see whether our gamble had paid off.

From the very first day, we ran out of space. The sixty seats were booked every lunchtime, and in the evenings when, in order to make things as casual as possible, we didn't take bookings, the restaurant would fill up by seven o'clock. The queues would continue all night and the bar heaved with happy people drinking Prosecco and Spritz.

The menu in POLPO is uncomplicated and the carefully researched dishes are all made with relatively few ingredients. There is no show-off cooking or complex technical artistry. The menu's appeal is that it keeps things simple. The most controversial thing you find on the menu is the addition of gremolata on the cuttlefish in its ink (the traditional recipe calls just for parsley). We have a rule that a dish is ready to put on the menu only when we have taken out as many ingredients as possible. As Antoine de Saint-Exupéry said: 'Perfection is achieved not when there is nothing more to add, but when there is nothing left to take away.'

Most of the recipes have only three or four ingredients (not counting stuff you would already have in your larder) and some require no cooking at all; they are easy but delicious exercises in assembly. If you want to cut corners, go ahead. If you want to smoke your own salmon or cure your own ham, good luck! But in my opinion, that's what delicatessens were invented for. One thing I will say is that you should always buy the best ingredients that you can afford. Your taste buds and your guests will thank you.

Because POLPO is a small-plate restaurant, all dishes are designed to be shared, but I have included conventional quantities so that you can adapt for first course and main course presentation too, if you choose. Sharing is a social activity, very Mediterranean and makes a meal more like a feast – a convivial experience. This was the philosophy that I lifted over the Dolomites, across the continent and planted in London.

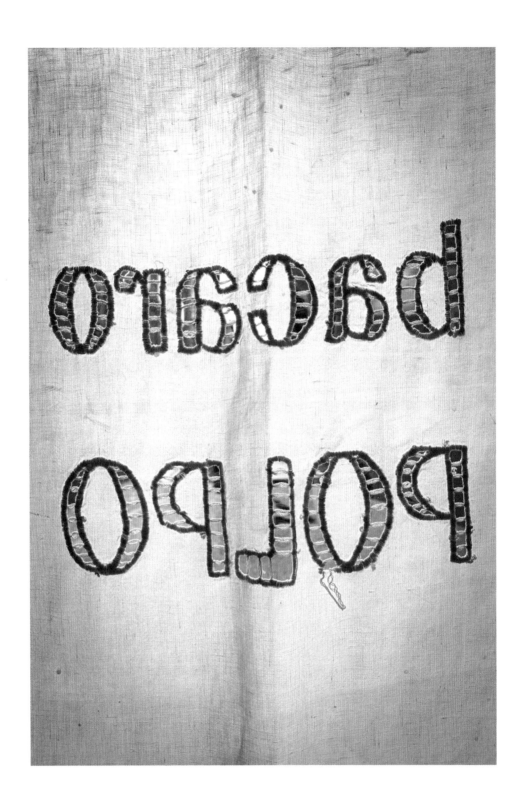

CICHÈTI

Bàcari are the closest thing that Venetians have to the British pub or the downtown New York bar. They are meeting places for locals, social hubs where you go for a drink or two. You will find politicians rubbing shoulders with market traders, gondoliers chatting to university professors, and the conversation will range from politics to football, nostalgia to gossip. Although they are unashamedly working-class, the bàcari differ from British pubs and New York bars in every other respect. In a pub the food tends to be dry and processed: potato crisps, roasted peanuts and pork scratchings. In Manhattan you'll get pretzels and nachos. In a bàcaro you will find cichèti.

Cichèti (the spelling is Venetian, in the rest of Italy they spell it cicchètti)* are small snacks, usually prepared in advance, that sit in a glass cabinet on the bar counter. They are often speared with a single toothpick to allow the barman to pick them up easily as you point to what you want. It's as simple as that. You wash your cichèto down with an ombra (literally a 'shadow', the word dates from when wines were placed in the shade to keep them cool) – a small glass of local wine.

These snacks can often be somewhat proletarian in their execution: a single anchovy from a tin wrapped around a single pickled onion stabbed with a toothpick, for example. Or they can be sublimely subtle like Baccalà Mantecato (boiled and flaked salt cod, infused with garlic and creamed with olive oil) on a lozenge of toast. Cichèti are not so far removed from what aspirational dinner party hostesses would call canapés. They are perfect to accompany a glass of wine or two, or to offset the seductive effects of a Spritz. They are also perfect as a way of whetting your guests' appetites. There is nothing like a little of what's to come to get the digestive juices flowing and the brain (and stomach) in gear for eating. As the Italians say: 'L'appetito vien mangiando' – with eating, comes appetite.

Often, cichèti use bread as their delivery mechanism. All the bàcari I have visited use a bought French stick sliced at an angle, sometimes toasted, often not, as the base for most of their cichèti. Some of the more serious modern osterie might use Pugliese (also bought) cut the same way. For the purposes of clarity, cichèti using little toasts as a base are referred to in the following section as crostini.

Crostini really are very simple indeed. The toasted discs of French stick, ciabatta, Pugliese (your choice) can be prepared in advance and you can add your topping twenty minutes or even half an hour before serving. This is so typically Venetian: bàcari have these hanging round in glass cabinets for half a day sometimes. You can 'reactivate' your little cichèti by adding a few drops of olive oil on vegetable and meat crostini or a few drops of lemon juice on the fishy ones.

Throughout the book, I have used Venetian dialect spellings where an ingredient, dish or term has a particular relevance or significance to Venice or the region.

I CICCHETTI

BACCALA
SARDE
TRIPPA
NERUETTI
POLPETTE
RADICCHIO
FOLPETTI
SAOR

PZ = 2,00/4,00 €

SARDÈLE IN SAÓR CROSTINI

The flavours in this simple dish, more than any other, define the taste of Venice for me. There is something very typical about the battle between sour and sweet, what Italians call 'agrodolce'. There are many different fish you can use to make this dish – including sprats or mackerel – but the most common are sardines, the smaller the better. Their oiliness, tangy flavour and generous flesh work so well when mixed with the sweet onions. This is such a good dish to make in a large batch and to keep in the fridge for up to a week. It is only ever eaten cold or, for best results, at room temperature.

For forty crostini:
500g small sardines
Seasoned Italian 00 flour
Extra virgin olive oil
100g pine nuts
4 large onions, finely sliced
400ml white wine vinegar
100g raisins, soaked overnight
Flaky sea salt
2 French sticks (or other bread)

Clean and gut the sardines. Take the heads and tails off. Give them a final rinse under running water and pat dry with kitchen towel. Coat in seasoned flour and shallow fry in olive oil until golden on both sides and then set aside.

Preheat the oven to 150°C/Gas 2. Place the pine nuts on a baking tray and toast in the oven for 10 minutes, or until lightly browned, shaking them about a couple of times. Set aside.

In a heavy-based pan sweat the sliced onion in olive oil on a medium-low heat for about 20–30 minutes, or until soft, sweet and translucent. Pour enough white wine vinegar over the onions to fully submerge. Make sure it's very wet – the fish will soak up a lot of the liquid. Drain the raisins and add along with the toasted pine nuts.

Lay some onion mix on the bottom of a large container and some sardines on top of this. Sprinkle small pinches of salt as you layer, but not too much – the vinegar adds quite a bit of sharpness. Alternate layers of onion and fish until all the sardines are used, cover and chill. This dish is better after a few days in liquid.

After a day or two, take as much of the mixture out of the fridge as you are going to use and leave for 30 minutes to bring up to room temperature. Cut your French stick, or other bread, on an angle and toast lightly. Dollop a generous amount onto each piece.

ANCHOVY &
CHICKPEA CROSTINI

*Our head chef Tom first had the idea for this dish in Croatia, which is only
an hour or so away from Venice by ferry.*

*The saltiness of the anchovy and the earthiness of the chickpeas here are
great bedfellows. It's another of those make-a-big-batch-and-keep-in-the-fridge
recipes that is just perfect for snacks. As humble as it is, this crostino causes
much comment at the restaurant because it is such a surprisingly tasty concoction.*

For ten crostini:
1 × 400g tin of chickpeas
10 brown anchovy fillets, plus some of their oil
Juice of ½ lemon
1 handful of flat parsley leaves, chopped
1 tablespoon tahini
Black pepper
About 4 tablespoons extra virgin olive oil
½ French stick (or other bread), sliced and lightly toasted

Drain and rinse the chickpeas and roughly chop the anchovies. Mix
together with the lemon juice, parsley and tahini. Add ½ teaspoon of
freshly ground black pepper. Pulse in a food processor, with a little
anchovy oil from the tin or bottle and enough olive oil to create a chunky
paste. Taste and adjust the seasoning (there is no need for salt).

You can use this straight away or put it in a covered container in the
fridge for up to a week, taking as much as you want to use out of the fridge
before serving to bring it to room temperature. To eat, spread roughly onto
lightly toasted slices of French stick.

CHOPPED CHICKEN LIVER CROSTINI

*Chopped liver is one of the great comfort foods and appears in the cooking
of many cultures. This version is a favourite; I particularly like the contrast
between the crunchy bread of the crostino and the smooth sweetness of the
chopped liver. This is another 'keeper' – make a big batch and keep in the fridge.
Covered with cling film or greaseproof paper, it will stay good for up to a week.*

For sixty crostini:
100ml olive oil, plus some more if necessary
3 large shallots, finely diced
2 garlic cloves, finely chopped
Flaky sea salt and pepper
1kg chicken livers, cleaned
Good splash (25ml) of brandy
Good splash (25ml) of port
2 hard-boiled eggs
3 French sticks (or other bread), sliced and lightly toasted

Pour half the olive oil into a heavy-based pan and sweat the diced shallots
and the garlic, seasoned with salt and pepper, over a very low heat. When
the shallots are translucent, remove the mixture from the pan and put to
one side. Pour in the rest of the olive oil, turn up the heat and add the
cleaned chicken livers. Season and cook until brown all over.

Take the pan off the heat, scrape the shallot mixture back into the pan
and use a potato masher to mix everything into a rough paste. Put
the pan back onto a medium heat and cook through with a good splash
of brandy and port.

Place the boiled eggs in a food processor and pulse. Add the liver mixture
and process till combined but not too smooth. Adjust the seasoning and
add more oil if necessary.

Spread the mixture liberally onto lightly toasted slices of French stick.

SMOKED SALMON, HORSERADISH & DILL CROSTINI

This is one of those assemblies that I never tire of. It's an easy, quick and efficient cichèto and doesn't require you to smoke your own salmon. Just make sure you buy the best smoked salmon you can afford.

For twenty crostini:
250g crème fraîche
2 tablespoons Dijon mustard
About 3 tablespoons freshly grated horseradish
    – or more if you like it hot
Flaky sea salt and black pepper
Pinch of caster sugar (optional)
1 French stick (or other bread), cut into discs and lightly toasted
500g thinly sliced smoked salmon
20 dill sprigs
Lemon juice

First make the horseradish cream by mixing together the crème fraîche, mustard and horseradish. Season with salt and pepper add a little caster sugar if the mixture is too tart.

Put a generous slice (about 25g) of smoked salmon on each piece of toasted French stick and top with a spoonful of the horseradish cream. Decorate each crostino with a sprig of dill. Add a few drops of lemon juice and a grinding of black pepper before serving.

PROSCIUTTO, MINT & FIG CROSTINI

Unless you have a slicing machine or have practised with one of those ferocious-looking knives you see in traditional Spanish tapas bars, you should ask your deli to slice the prosciutto for you. A good delicatessen will always ask you what weight or how many slices rather than 'How thick?' Supermarkets are very good at slicing pink processed sandwich-ham but are less adept at air-cured types. Prosciutto should always be so thin that it is almost transparent. If it disintegrates, it is too thin or too dry, but otherwise you want to be able to see light coming through the slices.

Figs are only really in season in Europe from mid- to late-summer, but you do find them later. They are an unusual fruit in that they do not ripen after they are picked so there is absolutely no point buying hard, unripe figs hoping they will ripen later. They will not. However, you can 'help' an under-ripe fig to soften and bring out its flavour by roasting it, quartered, with a little olive oil, salt, pepper and sugar for about 15 minutes at 140°C/Gas 1.

For any number:
French stick (or other bread), cut into discs
Extra virgin olive oil
Very thinly sliced prosciutto
Figs
Mint leaves
Flaky sea salt and black pepper

Toast and oil the bread, then lay on some prosciutto, a quarter of ripe fig and a single mint leaf. Secure with a toothpick. Sprinkle on a little salt and pepper and add a tiny drizzle of olive oil. This is a particularly pretty little crostino.

ROCKET & WALNUT PESTO CROSTINI

This little crostino packs a good flavour punch. The peppery rocket and earthy walnuts make a far more robust combination than basil and pine nuts, the more traditional ingredients in pesto. The sauce is great for many other purposes too, keeps for up to a week in the fridge and freezes well. Try it with linguine and even more grated Parmesan.

For twenty crostini:
300g rocket leaves
300g walnuts, roughly chopped
150g grated Parmesan
1½ tablespoons finely chopped garlic
Flaky sea salt and black pepper
Extra virgin olive oil
1 French stick (or other bread), sliced and lightly toasted

Make sure your rocket is dried well to remove any excess moisture. In a large bowl, mix the leaves with the chopped walnuts, Parmesan, finely chopped garlic and a good pinch of sea salt and ground black pepper.

Once the ingredients are combined, put half the mixture in a food processor. Pulse, slowly adding olive oil until the right consistency is achieved. You want this pesto to be thick enough to spread. Repeat with the other half. Now put the two batches together and check the seasoning.

Smear onto hot crunchy slices of toasted bread.

WHITE BEAN CROSTINI

White beans are one of those subtle flavours that we don't fully understand till we are older and wiser. The velvety texture of tender, puréed white beans here is really pleasing against the crunch of the crostino. If you find it difficult to get hold of cannellini you could try butter beans instead. If you are using tinned beans, drain and rinse under cold running water.

For twenty crostini:
150g dried cannellini beans (or 1 × 400g good quality tin,
     drained and rinsed)
1 onion, cut in half
2 bay leaves
Extra virgin olive oil
Juice and zest of ½ lemon
1 large garlic clove, finely chopped
1 handful of flat parsley leaves, roughly chopped
Flaky sea salt and black pepper
1 French stick (or other bread), sliced and lightly toasted

Soak the dried beans overnight. When soaked, drain them and place in a pan. Pour in enough fresh water to cover the beans by 5cm. Add the onion halves, bay leaves and a good glug of olive oil. Bring to the boil, skim off any scum that rises, turn down the heat and simmer until cooked (about 1–1½ hours).

When tender (or come in at this stage if using tinned white beans) remove half the beans and marinate with some more olive oil, the lemon juice and zest, the finely chopped garlic and the roughly chopped parsley, salt and pepper.

Purée the remaining beans in a food processor with enough olive oil so they reach a fluffy consistency a bit like hummus.

To serve, generously smear some of the purée onto the toasted bread and dress with the marinated beans.

TUNA & LEEK CROSTINI

This simple recipe earns its inclusion as it is one of the classic cichèti served at Cantinone già Schiavi, a famous bàcaro in Venice (see page 298). Alessandra is the matriarch who prepares all the food and serves it from a little counter throughout the day, every day. But despite the hard work and the relentless routine, she has still found the time to write her own recipe book. In the book she talks about making her first cichèto for her sons. This is it.

For twelve or so crostini:
1 × 200g tin of tuna in olive oil
80g mayonnaise
Brandy
Black pepper
1 French stick (or other bread), lightly toasted and oiled
1 leek

Mix the tuna with the mayonnaise and a splash of brandy and stir till you have a smooth paste. Season with black pepper – you may or may not need a little salt depending on your bread.

Spread onto slices of lightly toasted French stick or similar and then very finely slice the white portion of the leek into tiny ribbons. Scatter these onto the tuna mayonnaise and serve.

BACCALÀ MANTECATO

*Baccalà Mantecato is one of my Venetian 'Holy Grail' dishes. My quest
has taken some obsessive turns over the years; I have interrogated chefs and
restaurant owners as if compiling the gospels. I am in constant pursuit of the
purest expression of baccalà and seek out new places to test their recipes, hoping
that I am going to, one day, find the perfect version: my one true cod.*

*This dish is composed of dried salt cod that is soaked, softened, flaked,
infused with garlic and whipped into a cream with the slow addition of olive oil,
resulting in a white, fluffy, salty, fishy, garlicky soft paste. What could be
more delicious? Well, as it turns out, very few things. I have taken people
to Venice and watched their expressions change as they taste their first Baccalà
Mantecato. It helps to fully appreciate the 'wow' of this dish if you have tried
the real deal in Venice, and the best place to do that is at All'Arco near Rialto
Bridge (see page 310).*

*So first you need to find a good delicatessen selling dried salt cod. Spanish
delis seem to stock it as a matter of course. It looks like a small, thin cricket
bat. Then you need plenty of space for your stirring arms. This recipe is
daunting, and requires some practice to get it right (just like when you first made
mayonnaise), but it is incredibly rewarding once you are sat down with a slice of
warm crusty bread, spooning it on to eat your fifth mouthful...*

For at least forty crostini:
500ml garlic-infused, extra virgin olive oil – see below
12 garlic cloves, halved, plus 4 whole garlic cloves
1kg salt cod
About 1 litre milk
3 bay leaves
4 whole black peppercorns
1 small white onion, quartered
Fine salt and black pepper, if needed
2 French sticks (or other bread)

To make the garlic-infused oil, take a 1 litre bottle, half-filled with
extra virgin olive oil, and pop the 12 halved garlic cloves into it. Shake
occasionally. This can be used as and when needed, but is best after
48 hours.

Take your salt cod and place in a large container of cold water. Leave
to soak for at least 48 hours (depending on the saltiness of your cod) in
the fridge, covered, changing the water often. Taste a little bit of the cod.
When it has lost its overpowering taste of salt it is ready to prepare.

Place the cod in one layer in a wide pan. Pour over the milk (it should
just cover the cod; if not, add a little more). Add the bay leaves,

peppercorns, 4 whole garlic cloves and onion. Simmer gently for 20 minutes, or until the cod starts to fall apart. Remove from the heat immediately. Flake the cod, discarding any bones, into a warm mixing bowl. Pass the milk through a fine sieve and reserve.

Now, time for some exercise. Using the end of a rolling pin, pound the cod and add a little of the reserved milk – just enough to loosen the cod. Then slowly start adding the infused oil, continuously pounding to create a smooth, shiny paste. This should be a slow process, now gradually adding the oil while mixing with a wooden spoon, just like making mayonnaise. Taste it and add a little salt and pepper if needed.

Cut the bread on an angle and toast lightly. Spread the baccalà onto the warm toasts and serve.

ARANCINI

Arancini literally translates as 'small oranges' and they are traditionally made with yesterday's leftover risotto. Now I don't know about you, but in my experience there is no such thing as yesterday's leftover risotto; I find it impossible not to eat everything I make. If you are one of those enviable types who has willpower, then you can use whatever spare risotto you have in the fridge. If you're like me, you'll have to start from scratch.

It is important to note that when making risotto generally, it is always better to serve it 'al dente', that is, with a little bit of bite to the grains. But when you use leftover risotto, it has had more time to absorb more moisture and naturally will be softer. This is exactly the texture that works best for arancini. When cooking from scratch, you have to override your instinct to stop cooking at 'al dente' and cook the rice for a few moments more than normal.

For six arancini:
20ml olive oil
40g unsalted butter
1 zucchino, grated
1 medium shallot, finely diced
Flaky sea salt and black pepper
Leaves from 2 sprigs of thyme
500ml vegetable stock
100g risotto rice – carnaroli is best
½ glass of white wine
1 good handful of freshly grated Parmesan
½ × 150g ball of buffalo mozzarella
Instant polenta or fine cornmeal
1 litre vegetable oil, for deep-frying

Gently heat the olive oil and half the butter in a heavy-bottomed pan. Sweat the zucchino and diced shallot and add salt and pepper. Stir in the thyme. Meanwhile, heat the vegetable stock up in another saucepan.

When the shallots turn translucent, add the rice and gently heat, stirring, for 5 minutes on a low flame. You want to make sure that every grain is coated and shiny but the rice and vegetables must not turn brown. Add the white wine at this stage. When the wine has been absorbed, add the hot vegetable stock, one ladle at a time, making sure the rice is always submerged, stirring gently from time to time. When the rice is fully cooked (about 15–20 minutes), finish with a handful of grated Parmesan and the rest of the butter. Check that the rice is well seasoned.

Take the pan off the heat and spread the risotto onto flat plates or a tray to cool. Cut the mozzarella into little cubes.

When the rice is cool, roll into golf-ball-sized spheres with a cube of mozzarella in the middle. Roll each ball in the polenta or cornmeal and deep-fry until golden brown (usually about 2–3 minutes). Don't be afraid of deep-frying, even if you are not used to it. Simply put a litre of vegetable oil so it half fills a deep pan and bring the temperature up to 190°C (or until a cube of bread dropped in the oil turns golden in less than a minute). Use tongs or a slotted spoon to move the arancini around and drain them on kitchen paper.

You need to serve your arancini immediately. They don't last long and are disappointing when cold. You want the mozzarella to be really stringy when the little balls are bitten into. For a bit of fun, skewer each with a toothpick and serve them like small lollipops.

MOZZARELLA BOCCONCINI

Bocconcini translates as 'small mouthfuls'. These are great fun as canapés or made in a batch and put onto your dinner table just as your guests arrive. Children love them because they are very tasty and the stringy cheese sometimes stretches to comical lengths. Like the arancini, you can serve these on a toothpick, lollipop-style.

Panko, if you haven't used it before, is a very handy breadcrumb mix that you can pick up in oriental supermarkets.

For six bocconcini:
80g panko breadcrumbs
Zest of 1 lemon
1 handful of oregano leaves, chopped
Italian 00 flour, salted
1 medium free-range egg, beaten
1 × 125g ball of buffalo mozzarella, cut into 6 chunks
1 litre vegetable oil, for deep-frying

Prepare your coating mix by combining the panko breadcrumbs with the zest and oregano. Put the salted flour on one plate and the beaten egg in a shallow bowl. Take a piece of mozzarella, roll in the salted flour, then in the beaten egg, then the panko mix (you may have some panko mix left over). Repeat with the other pieces. You can do this a few hours or the morning before cooking and chill until needed.

Half fill a deep pan with the vegetable oil and bring it up to 190°C (or until a cube of bread dropped in the oil turns golden in less than a minute). Deep-fry the coated mozzarella until golden brown. Drain on kitchen paper and serve hot.

POTATO & PARMESAN CROCCHETTE

Croquettes (crocchette in Italian) get a bad name in Venice. There are neat little varieties you can buy frozen in the supermarket that unscrupulous bars and bàcari deep-fry and offer as cichèti. Bad form! You can usually spot them a mile off as they are perfectly spherical and glow an unnaturally luminous yellow. But when you come across crocchette that are properly made with good ingredients, they are in a different league.

For twelve crocchette:
4 medium floury potatoes, such as King Edward or Maris Piper
125g grated Parmesan
1 medium free-range egg, beaten
Flaky sea salt and black pepper
1 litre vegetable oil
Instant polenta or fine cornmeal
1 lemon, cut into 6 wedges

Scrub the potatoes clean and boil in their skins until cooked. When cool enough to handle, peel and grate coarsely (you can peel the potato first but they have more flavour this way). Add the grated Parmesan and the egg then season with salt and pepper.

Half fill a deep pan with the vegetable oil and start to heat it up. You want it to be 190°C. (You can test this by dropping a cube of bread into the oil; it should turn golden in less than a minute.) Meanwhile, shape the mixture into 12 slightly elongated balls, like really short sausages. Roll in polenta or cornmeal and deep-fry for 2 minutes until golden. Drain on kitchen paper and serve hot, with a lemon wedge.

CAPRESE STACK

The combination of three good ingredients and nothing else. This is an abbreviation of the mighty Insalata Caprese (see page 197), but gives you all the essentials in one single mouthful.

Take a little piece of mozzarella, half a small tomato (the best quality you can find, ripe and at room temperature, please) and a leaf of basil. Spear them together with a wooden toothpick and sprinkle with salt flakes, a grinding of black pepper and a few drops of olive oil. If you prepare them in advance, leave the sprinkle of salt, pepper and drizzle of olive oil until just before you serve them. This sort of 'reactivates' the stacks. Make sure they are not fridge-cold as this will mask the flavours.

CICHÈTI

MORTADELLA CUBE

Mortadella is so comically, artificially pink and spotty that many 'serious' cooks give it a wide berth. But it is ubiquitous in the delis and wine bars of Venice and I believe it to be an underrated ingredient. The use of Emmental in this snack is not so incongruous as it seems; much of northern Italian cooking has been influenced by what goes on across the mountains in Switzerland and Austria. (In fact, the Italian region of Alto Adige which borders Veneto was Austrian until as recently as 1919 when it was annexed by Italy.)

This is a very simple cichèto that evokes the 1970s classic served at suburban dinner parties: pineapple chunk with cheese.

Buy your mortadella as a whole piece rather than sliced. Cut it into cubes the size of large dice. Take a green pitted olive, wrap a small thin sheet of Emmental cheese around it and then push a wooden toothpick through and into the mortadella cube. Season with black pepper.

ARTICHOKE & SPECK

Tinned artichokes are incredibly common in northern Italian kitchens and there is nothing wrong with using them in yours. You will find them in good Italian delis. Speck is smoked ham flavoured with juniper found extensively in northern Italy, particularly Alto Adige. However, speck in Germany and Austria means the fatty white ham that Italians call lardo. Very confusing. When you buy your speck, ask for it sliced thinly.

Take a single artichoke; tightly wrap a small sheet of speck around it and skewer with a wooden toothpick. Once again, a little salt and olive oil will 'reactivate' if you prepare these in advance.

GRISSINI, PICKLED RADICCHIO & SALAMI

These little cichèti are like savoury lollipops. I can't imagine any other way of persuading bambini to eat pickled radicchio. Since you are buying the salami and the breadsticks, the only part you need to prepare is the pickled radicchio. When buying breadsticks, choose the slightly more expensive Italian grissini rather than the thick moulded ones; or make your own (see page 100).

For twenty grissini:
200ml white wine
200ml white wine vinegar
4 juniper berries
20 leaves of radicchio
Extra virgin olive oil
20 grissini
20 thin slices of salami

Bring the white wine and the white wine vinegar to the boil with the juniper berries. When the liquid is bubbling, submerge the radicchio leaves for 5 minutes.

Take off the heat, remove the radicchio with tongs and gently shake off any excess liquid. Keep the pickled leaves covered in olive oil. When you are ready to use them, simply take out the leaves and drain them slightly of any excess oil.

Wrap the top end of the grissini with a piece of pickled radicchio and a slice of salami.

FRIED STUFFED OLIVES

These cunning little savoury confections surprise and delight with the first bite. You're not really sure what to expect, but the double hit of saltiness from the olive and then the anchovy tends to wake up the taste buds and sharpen the appetite. They're as sophisticated a cocktail snack as any I know and never fail to impress.

For twenty olives:
10 brown anchovy fillets, drained
5 sage leaves
1 garlic clove
Juice of ½ lemon
Black pepper
1 handful of grated Parmesan
20 large Italian 'queen' green olives, pitted
3 medium free-range egg whites
Italian 00 flour for coating
Panko breadcrumbs (you can buy these in oriental supermarkets)
1 litre vegetable oil

Chop the anchovies, sage and garlic as finely as possible and then, using a pestle and mortar (or in a bowl with the end of a rolling pin), turn into a paste, adding the lemon juice a few drops at a time. Mix in a pinch of black pepper and the Parmesan.

Stuff the olives by using a disposable piping bag to squirt your mixture into the hole left from pitting the olives. Dip into the egg white, then the flour, and then the breadcrumbs.

Half fill a deep pan with the vegetable oil and bring the temperature up to 190°C (or until a cube of bread dropped in the oil turns golden in less than a minute). Deep-fry the coated olives in the oil for 2–3 minutes, or until golden brown. Drain on kitchen paper.

GRILLED FENNEL & WHITE ANCHOVY SKEWERS

One of the oldest and most atmospheric bàcari in Venice is Do Mori (see page 310). It is positioned between two narrow calle close to the Rialto fish market and its long, dark bar fills up with market traders shortly after 11am every market day morning. It was here that I first learnt about assembly. The glass cabinets are lined with cichèti where pretty much any two complementary ingredients are fused together by being skewered on a toothpick. It's a great technique: the skewers are easy for you to pick up and eat but also easy for the Venetian bartenders to handle hygienically and put onto your plate.

This little cichèto follows the two-ingredients-on-a-toothpick method and these two strong flavours work very well together. Grilling the fennel helps to heighten its lovely aniseed qualities.

For ten skewers:
1 small fennel bulb
Extra virgin olive oil
Flaky sea salt
1 handful of roughly chopped dill fronds
10 white anchovy fillets

Preheat your oven grill to medium. Slice the fennel bulb through the root into medium-thin sections around 5mm thick. Place the slices onto a baking tray and drizzle with a little olive oil. Add a few pinches of salt, half the dill and toss a few times to coat. Place the baking tray under the preheated grill, turning over once, for 10–15 minutes, or until the fennel is starting to brown at the edges. Remove and set aside.

When the fennel has cooled enough to handle, take a single white anchovy fillet and skewer it together with a single piece of grilled fennel. You can then arrange your cichèti on a plate, scatter over the remaining dill and serve.

MORTADELLA, WALNUT & GORGONZOLA WRAP

This style of cichèto is less prevalent in Venice but very popular in POLPO. Because you are wrapping a piece of ham, beef or thinly sliced fish around your other ingredients, there is no need for the lozenge of toast or polenta underneath. It's occasionally nice to do without the starch.

This slightly sinful combination of creamy cheese, salty cheese and sweet ham is given a virtuous crunch by the walnuts.

For sixteen wraps:
300g soft Gorgonzola
100g mascarpone
2 handfuls of roughly chopped walnuts
Black pepper
16 very thin, circular slices of mortadella

Combine the Gorgonzola and the mascarpone into a stiff, creamy paste. Add the chopped walnuts and a grind of pepper. In weight terms, you need about 2:1 cheese to nuts.

Put two heaped teaspoons of the mixture into a slice of mortadella and wrap it up like you're rolling a thick cigarette – about the thickness of a finger. Skewer with a wooden toothpick. Repeat for the rest of the slices. Arrange your wraps on a plate and serve.

BRESAOLA, ROCKET & PARMESAN WRAP

Bresaola is air-cured beef and readily available these days. It has a lovely firm texture that is more robust than, say, prosciutto and holds this wrap together particularly well. It is a deep reddish brown and looks great against the shiny green rocket leaves.

For sixteen wraps:
1 large handful of washed and dried rocket leaves
Lemon juice
Extra virgin olive oil
Flaky sea salt
150g Parmesan, shaved
16 thin slices of bresaola

Dress the rocket with a little lemon juice, some olive oil and salt. Add shavings of Parmesan and mix thoroughly. Roll up in slices of bresaola and skewer with a wooden toothpick.

SMOKED SALMON, RICOTTA & DILL WRAP

Another starchless cichèto with a delicate balance of flavours that is light enough to serve with pre-dinner drinks. The sharpness of the lemon zest and the aromatic dill really get your taste buds jumping. (The best type of zester to use here is the little gadget that looks like a tiny knuckleduster.)

For sixteen wraps:
300g soft ricotta
Zest and juice of 1 lemon
1 handful of dill, chopped, plus a little extra to serve
Flaky sea salt and black pepper
16 thin slices of smoked salmon

Combine the ricotta, lemon zest and chopped dill. Mix well with a spoon and season with salt and pepper.

Place one large teaspoonful of the mixture onto a thin slice of salmon and roll up to about the size of your little finger. Skewer with a wooden toothpick. Repeat for the rest of the salmon and arrange on a plate. Before serving, squeeze on a few drops of lemon juice and garnish with dill.

AUBERGINE
& PARMESAN WRAP

Aubergine is such a meaty vegetable (or fruit, to be really pedantic) that it is often useful as an alternative to meat if you are feeling less carnivorous. Unlike the other wraps in this section, this one requires a little cooking but it is definitely worth the effort.

For twenty or more wraps:
2 long purple aubergines, trimmed
Extra virgin olive oil
Flaky sea salt and black pepper
150ml tomato sauce – see page 149
1 large handful of grated Parmesan
1 large handful of grated mozzarella – the cheap, hard kind
1 handful of basil leaves

Heat up a griddle pan and an oven grill. Slice the aubergines lengthways into 5mm sheets. Brush with olive oil, season and place on a hot griddle pan for 2 minutes each side.

Lay the aubergines on an oiled baking tray. Smear onto each slice 1 tablespoon of the tomato sauce, some grated Parmesan, some grated mozzarella and 2 leaves of basil. Lightly grill to melt the cheese, leave for a few moments to cool slightly and then roll up.

These can be served later at room temperature but do not refrigerate well. It's best to eat them straight away, or while they're still warm, drizzled with a little olive oil.

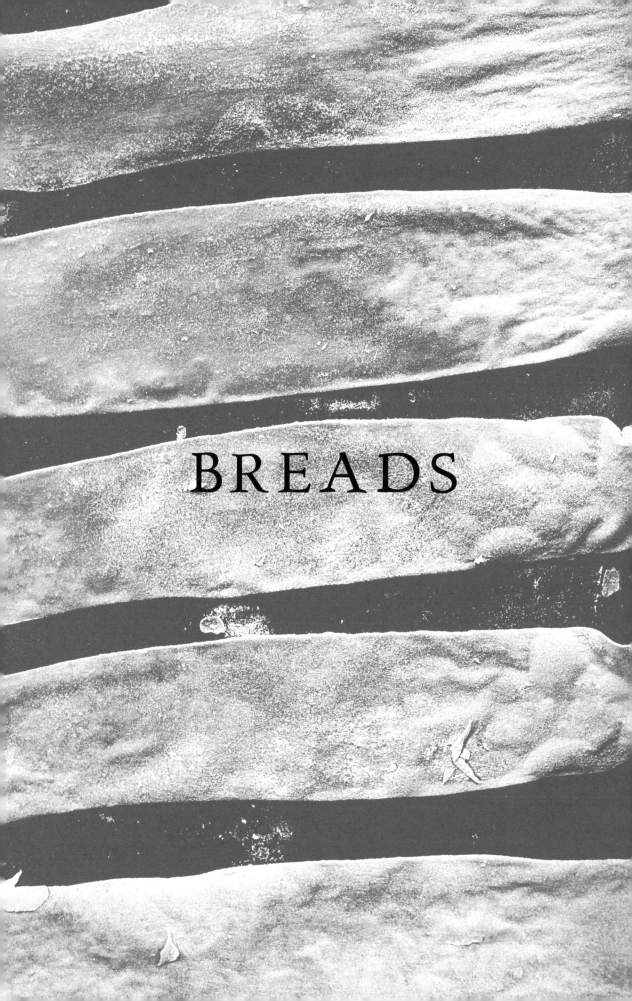

BREADS

I love the Italian attitude to bread. You make it, you eat it, you get on with it. It is an attitude that is straightforward, no-nonsense and born of necessity; none of the fuss and reverence that you find in the artisanal approach of some New York or London bakeries I know. In Italy, it is taken for granted that good food deserves good bread.

Most restaurants I have visited in Italy rely on the local baker to provide the bread required for their cichèti, crostini, bruschette and panini. This way they can ensure quality and consistency. That doesn't mean you have to buy yours too, however. This section contains recipes for all the breads we enjoy making on a daily basis in our small Soho kitchen. If you have the time, you should have a go. There are very few things more satisfying than making your own bread. But if you don't have time, there is no shame at all in buying good quality bread from a professional baker and using that instead.

The one dough that you really must make yourself, however, is pizza dough. It is very simple and opens up a world of possibilities. So it is such a shame that pizza has become the ubiquitous, mass-produced fast food that we see on take-away menus pushed through our letterboxes and stacked high in the freezer cabinets of supermarkets. Some of the flavour combinations are so strange that I often find myself shaking my head slowly as I read the descriptions.

In Venice, many of these crimes are perpetrated on a daily basis at the depressing tourist traps where waiters wear striped gondolier shirts and occasionally sing Neapolitan ditties. No wonder the city's cuisine has such a bad name.

But I have had delightful pizza in Italy and in many places outside Italy too. The best ones are always the simplest. Pizza needs a very thin base and sparse topping. Just as with any other dish, the combination of ingredients should be balanced, subtle and complementary. Less is more.

PIZZA OR PIZZETTA
BASE DOUGH

When you make pizza at home it is unlikely you will have a wood-fired oven. These ovens generate a temperature of around 300°C, the sort of heat you would expect in a commercial pizza oven. But even a domestic oven can manage a healthy 250°C, and there is a way you can give it a little help: treat yourself to a pizza stone. You'll find these in cookware shops and good department stores, or you could make your own by getting an appropriately sized 2–3cm-thick piece of unpolished granite from a stonemason. You simply place your pizza stone on the middle shelf in your oven. When your oven reaches 250°C/Gas 9, so will your stone and the heat will distribute effectively and evenly to the base of your pizza. Otherwise, make sure you put a baking sheet in the oven to heat up instead. You'll also find it much easier to handle the raw pizza base (and its topping) with a pizza blade or 'peel'. If you don't have one, use a spatula or fish slice.

Now, a word on size. We make pizzette, which are slightly smaller than pizza, about 20cm in diameter rather than 30cm. As well as being prettier and faster, this size is also more convenient – you might get 2 or 3 pizzette onto your pizza stone rather than a single large one.

We use fresh yeast, which you can find in health food shops, bakeries and even by asking at the bakery departments of some supermarkets. Otherwise use sachets of fast-action dried yeast.

For twelve pizzetta bases:
15g fresh yeast (or 1 × 7g sachet fast-action yeast)
300ml tepid water
500g strong white flour – Italian 00 is good
15g (2 teaspoons) fine salt
2 tablespoons extra virgin olive oil

Whisk together the fresh yeast (if using) and the water. You can make cold water tepid by adding a splash from a boiled kettle.

In a large bowl, mix the flour, salt and dried yeast (if using) with the olive oil and the yeasty (or plain) water and form the mixture into a ball.

Now knead the dough on a floured work surface. To do this, push the dough backwards and forwards simultaneously with your two hands so that you are stretching it and then pushing it back down into a ball. Repeat this, giving the dough a good working over. You shouldn't break into a sweat but it should feel like a little work-out for your hands and forearms, and you should be feeling the dough getting more and more springy. After 10 minutes of kneading, push the dough back into a ball,

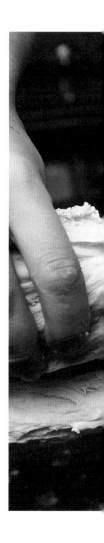

flour the top, place in a bowl and cover with oiled clingfilm. Leave to rise in a warm place.

After at least 30 minutes, but ideally when doubled in size, your dough is ready. Divide the dough into 12 large golf-ball-sized pieces and then roll them into thin 20cm discs. Top with the rest of your ingredients and cook. If you want to use the dough later, place the balls of dough on a tray, cover with a damp cloth and leave in the fridge for up to 12 hours. Just remember to take them out 30 minutes before you're ready to use them.

Remember that your pizza will benefit from being placed directly onto a hot baking sheet or pizza stone within a preheated oven – our pizzas take no longer than 5 minutes. At 250°C, yours will take about 6–8 minutes.

Finally, please don't worry about getting totally round and even bases for your pizzette. In fact, it's much better if they are not; you'll get some lovely bubbling and occasional charring.

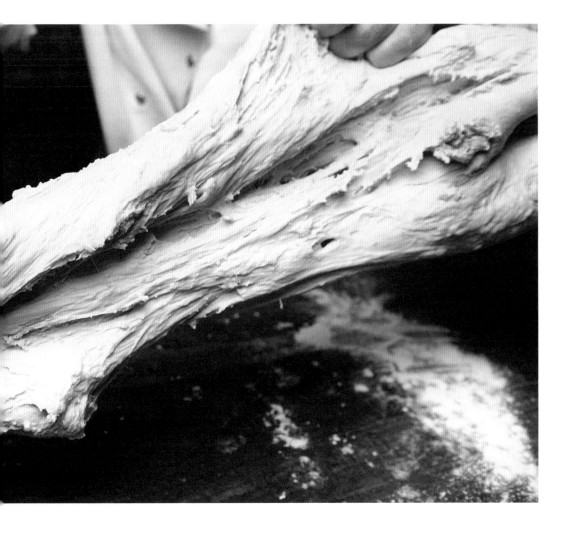

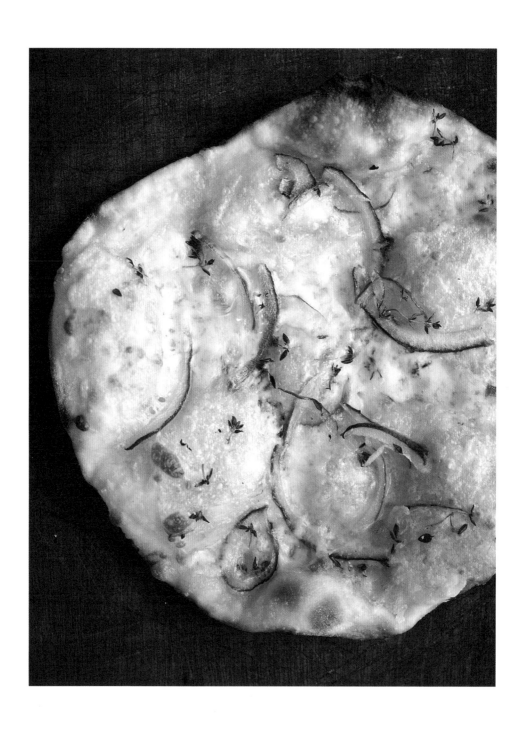

PIZZETTA BIANCA

*This simple pizzetta is a variation on the classic Roman Pizza Bianca
(not really a pizza at all, more like flatbread with olive oil, rosemary and salt).
Our version has two white cheeses and thyme. It is so fragrant and pungent that
it turns heads as it is taken through the restaurant. 'What was that?', everyone
asks. They always order one for themselves.*

*In this instance, it is better to use dense, cheap mozzarella rather than
expensive moist buffalo varieties. The cheaper stuff is very easy to grate and
has less water content and therefore melts better.*

For one pizzetta:
1 large golf-ball-sized piece of pizza dough – see page 62
1 small handful of grated block mozzarella
1 small handful of grated Parmesan
¼ small red onion, thinly sliced
About 12–15 picked thyme leaves
Black pepper
Extra virgin olive oil

Preheat your oven to its highest setting (250°C/Gas 9 or above). At
the same time put a pizza stone or baking sheet in the oven to heat up.

Roll the pizza base out to around 20cm in diameter. Evenly distribute
the cheeses, the onion and almost all of the thyme over the pizza base.
Be sparing – a little goes a long way. If you use too much topping
the base won't be crisp enough. Around 6 minutes on a pizza stone
should do for this one. Don't burn the cheese.

Just before serving, grind on some pepper, sprinkle over a little olive
oil and scatter over the remaining thyme leaves.

SPINACH, SOFT EGG & PARMESAN PIZZETTA

I don't know the first incidence of a runny egg on top of a pizza but whoever had the idea deserves a medal. It's a glorious moment when you cut into the centre of the pizza and the yolk breaks and oozes yellow onto the plate. The base for this pizzetta needs a bit of practice – you want the dough and filling to be slightly thicker at the edges to prevent the egg from running over the sides.

For one pizzetta:
1 very large handful of spinach
1 tablespoon crème fraîche
¼ garlic clove, finely chopped
1 small handful of grated Parmesan
Flaky sea salt and black pepper
1 large golf-ball-sized piece of pizza dough – see page 62
1 small free-range egg

Preheat your oven to its highest setting (250°C/Gas 9 or above). At the same time put a pizza stone or baking sheet in the oven to heat up.

Now you need to blanch your spinach. Take a very large handful (spinach reduces in volume dramatically when cooked) and plunge the leaves into boiling salted water for one minute. Remove the spinach and plunge into ice-cold water. Squeeze dry and finely chop what will now be a smaller handful. Add the crème fraîche, garlic, about three-quarters of the Parmesan, a pinch of salt and a grind of pepper. Mix together to form a deep-green paste.

Roll the dough out to around 20cm in diameter. Evenly spread the spinach mixture over the pizza base making sure it is slightly raised at the edges, creating a tiny wall. Crack an egg into the centre and place on your pizza stone in the oven for 6–8 minutes. One minute before your pizza is ready, sprinkle over the remaining Parmesan and a grinding of black pepper.

Please don't overcook. It is essential that the egg is runny when served.

ZUCCHINO, MINT
& CHILLI PIZZETTA

Zucchini are definitely underrated. They take on an elegant quality when thinly sliced and look very pretty in cross-section, as used here. The simple effect of the heat from the chilli and the cooling mint makes this a really successful ensemble.

For one pizzetta:
1 large golf-ball-sized piece of pizza dough – see page 62
1 small handful of grated block mozzarella – the hard, cheap kind
1 small handful of grated Parmesan
½ zucchino
½ red chilli, deseeded and finely sliced
Flaky sea salt and black pepper
Extra virgin olive oil
4–6 mint leaves, roughly chopped

Preheat your oven to its highest setting (250°C/Gas 9 or above). At the same time put a pizza stone or baking sheet in the oven to heat up.

Roll the dough out to around 20cm in diameter. Evenly distribute a small amount of Parmesan and mozzarella – just enough to cover the pizza. Finely slice the zucchino to cover the cheese (use a mandoline or a potato peeler) and sprinkle with some finely sliced red chilli. Season and drizzle with olive oil.

Place the pizzetta on your stone or baking sheet in your preheated oven for about 6–8 minutes and garnish with some roughly chopped mint and a drizzle of olive oil.

STRACCHINO, POTATO & ROSEMARY PIZZETTA

It is quite surprising to some people to see potatoes on pizza but it's a common Italian marriage and works brilliantly, particularly here with potato's favourite bedfellow, rosemary. Stracchino is readily available in Italian delis and is a very mild and soft cows' milk cheese. It is normally sold in a slab and the taste reminds me (dare I say it) of spreadable cheese from a tube.

For one pizzetta:
2 Pink Fir potatoes (or other waxy variety)
1 large golf-ball-sized piece of pizza dough – see page 62
1 tablespoon stracchino
1 small handful of grated block mozzarella – the hard, cheap kind
Leaves from a sprig of rosemary
Extra virgin olive oil
Flaky sea salt

Preheat your oven to its highest setting (250°C/Gas 9 or above). At the same time put a pizza stone or baking sheet in the oven to heat up.

Slice the potatoes very thinly and blanch in boiling water for 30 seconds. Rinse immediately in cold water. Roll the dough out to around 20cm in diameter. Spread the stracchino onto the dough base and scatter on the potatoes. Now add the grated mozzarella and rosemary leaves.

Cook on the pizza stone or baking sheet in your preheated oven for 6–8 minutes, remove, drizzle with a little olive oil and a good crunch of salt flakes.

ASPARAGUS, TALEGGIO & SPECK PIZZETTA

Taleggio is one of those cheeses with a smell that announces its arrival before you see it. It has a strong and pungent aroma but a reasonably mild and fruity flavour. Its soft and yielding texture means that it melts particularly well, too. We love using Taleggio as a base for pizza and it works marvellously with asparagus and speck; the sweetness of the cheese contrasts with the salty tang of the smoked ham.

Speck is a cold-smoked, de-boned ham and is available in good Italian delicatessens. You should ask for it to be sliced very thinly indeed.

For one pizzetta:
2 asparagus spears
1 large golf-ball-sized piece of pizza dough – see page 62
1 small handful of grated block mozzarella – the hard, cheap kind
1 small handful of grated Taleggio
3 very thin slices of speck
Extra virgin olive oil
Black pepper

Preheat your oven to its highest setting (250°C/Gas 9 or above). At the same time put a pizza stone or baking sheet in the oven to heat up.

Blanch the asparagus spears in salted boiling water for 2 minutes. Remove them and plunge into ice cold water for a minute before slicing each of the spears into 5 pieces on the diagonal.

Roll out the dough to around 20cm in diameter. Evenly distribute the cheeses over the base. Scatter the cut asparagus pieces onto the surface. Place the pizzetta on the pizza stone or baking sheet in your very hot oven for around 5–7 minutes.

When the pizza is done, lay the thinly sliced speck over the top with a few folds to create some height and just before serving, sprinkle a little olive oil onto the surface and grind over a little pepper.

PORK & PICKLED PEPPER PIZZETTA

We had great fun naming this one. Although the main ingredient is coppa (cured pork shoulder), we decided to describe it on the menu as the tongue-twisting 'Pork & Pickled Pepper Pizzetta'. Unlike the pizzas you find in most pizzerias, ours at POLPO are mostly made without a tomato base. This recipe is one exception.

It is completely acceptable to use passata from a jar (it is, after all, one of the advantages of modern civilization).

For one pizzetta:
1 large golf-ball-sized piece of pizza dough – see page 62
2 tablespoons passata
1 handful of grated Parmesan
2–3 very thin slices of coppa
2 pickled jalapeño peppers, thinly sliced (you can get these in jars
    at your deli or in good supermarkets)
Extra virgin olive oil

Preheat your oven to its highest setting (250°C/Gas 9 or above). At the same time put a pizza stone or baking sheet in the oven to heat up.

Roll out the dough into a 20cm disc. Spread the pizzetta base with the passata. Lightly sprinkle with some grated Parmesan and lay the thinly sliced coppa on top of the sauced base. Sprinkle over a little more Parmesan and the thinly sliced pickled peppers.

Pop the pizzetta into the preheated oven on your pizza stone or baking sheet for 8 minutes or so. Add a few drops of olive oil before serving.

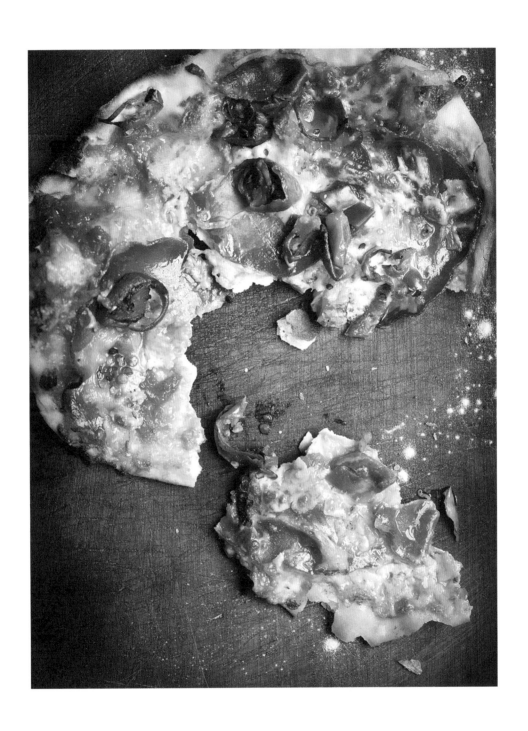

OLIVE & WHITE ANCHOVY PIZZETTA

It is important that you use white anchovies for this pizzetta. They are available at most delicatessens and even at supermarket deli counters. They are sometimes labelled as marinated white anchovies. In Spanish delis they are called boquerones. Do not be tempted to use the tinned brown variety – not the same at all.

For one pizzetta:
1 large golf-ball-sized piece of pizza dough – see page 62
1 handful of grated block mozzarella – the hard, cheap kind
5–6 pitted green olives, halved
5 white anchovy fillets – at room temperature, not straight
    from the fridge
5 basil leaves, roughly torn
Extra virgin olive oil

Preheat your oven to its highest setting (250°C/Gas 9 or above). At the same time put a pizza stone or baking sheet in the oven to heat up.

Roll out the pizza dough into a rough 20cm disc. Lightly sprinkle the base with mozzarella and evenly scatter over the olives. Cook on the pizza stone or baking sheet in your preheated oven for 6–8 minutes and remove from oven. Garnish with the anchovy fillets and torn basil leaves. Lightly drizzle with olive oil before serving.

MORTADELLA, GORGONZOLA & PICKLED RADICCHIO PIZZETTA

Mortadella is the pink ham with big white circles and is mild and firm-textured. It is flavoured with, among other things, myrtle berries. In fact, the Romans called it myrtle sausage. It complements the salty Gorgonzola and sharp radicchio really well and takes on an almost sweet quality when warmed. Don't be put off by its bright artificial colour — it is used widely in Venetian bàcari, and with good reason.

For one pizzetta:
1 large golf-ball-sized piece of pizza dough — see page 62
1 small handful of crumbled Gorgonzola
1 small handful of grated block mozzarella — the hard, cheap kind
4 thin slices of mortadella
4 leaves of pickled radicchio — see page 48 in the recipe for
    Grissini, Pickled Radicchio & Salami
Lemon juice

Preheat your oven to its highest setting (250°C/Gas 9 or above). At the same time put a pizza stone or baking sheet in the oven to heat up.

Roll out the dough into a rough 20cm disc. Spread the cheeses evenly on the base. Lay on the slices of mortadella and intersperse them with the pickled radicchio leaves.

Cook on a pizza stone in your preheated oven for 6–8 minutes. Squeeze a few drops of lemon juice on the mortadella before serving.

PROSCIUTTO & ROCKET PIZZETTA

You must make sure that your delicatessen understands that you want your prosciutto sliced very thinly indeed. The flavour will be so much more apparent, the ham almost melting as you press it between your tongue and the roof of your mouth.

Rocket is a leaf that can sometimes be over-represented on restaurant menus, but used in moderation it is lovely, strong and has a brilliant pepperiness. I quite like to grab this pizzetta, fold it in half, and eat it like a sandwich. I've always been common.

For one pizzetta:
1 large golf-ball-sized piece of pizza dough – see page 62
2 tablespoons passata
1 handful of grated block mozzarella – the hard, cheap kind
1 handful of rocket leaves
Juice of ½ lemon
Extra virgin olive oil
3 very thin slices of prosciutto

Preheat your oven to its highest setting (250°C/Gas 9 or above). At the same time put a pizza stone or baking sheet in the oven to heat up.

Roll out the dough into a rough 20cm disc. Spread the base with the passata and then sprinkle lightly with grated mozzarella. Put onto your pizza stone or baking sheet in your preheated oven for about 6–8 minutes.

Lightly dress the rocket leaves in the lemon juice and a little olive oil. Lay the slices of prosciutto across the pizzetta the moment you take it out of the oven. Put the dressed rocket on top.

MUSHROOM PIADINA

Piadina is a flatbread from Romagna and is usually sold on the street from little stalls with a variety of toppings. The flatbread is cooked on a hot stone or a grill, sometimes in a pan, and folded around the topping so that the whole thing can be picked up and eaten on-the-go. The term is an affectionate derivation of the flatbread called piada and it doesn't take a huge leap of imagination to connect this word to the pitta of North Africa and the pide of Turkey. Giovanni Pascoli writes about these lovely flatbreads in his saucily tongue-in-cheek 1900 poem 'La Piada'.

> *Ma tu, Maria, con le tue mani blande domi la pasta e poi l'allarghi e spiani;*
> *ed ecco è liscia come un foglio, e grande come la luna;*
> *e sulle aperte mani tu me l'arrechi,*
> *e me l'adagi molle sul testo caldo, e quindi t'allontani.*
> *Io, la giro, e le attizzo con le molle il fuoco sotto,*
> *fin che stride invasa dal calor mite, e si rigonfia in bolle:*
> *e l'odore del pane empie la casa.*

> *But you, Maria, with your soft hands, you tame the dough and stretch it flat;*
> *And now it is as smooth as paper, and as large as the moon;*
> *Then you spread it over my outstretched hands,*
> *And I lay it gently on the hot surface, and you stand back.*
> *I flip it up, and with the poker I awake the fire below,*
> *So that the intense heat makes it blister:*
> *And the smell of bread fills the house.*

Wouldn't it be great if all recipes could be written like this? Here is my more prosaic version.

For one piadina:
1 large golf-ball-sized piece of pizza dough – see page 62
Extra virgin olive oil
1 handful of good sliced mushrooms – Portobello are perfect
Flaky sea salt and black pepper
½ garlic clove, finely chopped
1 handful of flat parsley leaves, roughly chopped

Follow the recipe for pizza dough on page 62. When it comes to rolling out the dough to the right size, you carry on a little bit. Your individual piadina should be slightly larger than a 20cm pizzetta base; in other words, it needs to be super-thin.

Heat a large griddle pan on your stove with a little olive oil. Or if you've got a barbecue fired up, even better. Place the piadina on top

for 15 seconds each side and repeat if necessary. You want the bread to start to darken, maybe to blister in places, perhaps get a little burnt on one edge.

Sauté the mushrooms in olive oil, with a pinch of salt and a grind of pepper, on a high temperature for about 1½ minutes, or until the mushrooms give out their moisture. Add the chopped garlic and roughly chopped parsley and cook for about 1 minute more. Remove from the heat and roll the mushrooms up in your just-cooked piadina or fold the piadina to make a pocket and fill with the mixture instead.

TOMATO BRUSCHETTE

I have been making bruschette since I was a student and really couldn't cook. If you can make toast, you can make a bruschetta. It's a simple and effective preparation that is so flexible and adaptable that I think it could probably take any topping and still be great.

You need to get the right bread. At POLPO we use our homemade focaccia, but only because it is there. At home I use soda bread or sourdough. These are ideal. If you have a farmers' market nearby, or a good baker, food hall or decent supermarket, then you should be able to get a large sourdough loaf. Failing that, any hard-crusted, round country-style loaf should do the trick. If you can't get any of the above, even the lowliest supermarkets have little individual ciabatta in cellophane. They will have to do.

For two bruschette:
2–3 really good ripe tomatoes
1 small handful of basil leaves, torn
Extra virgin olive oil
Flaky sea salt and black pepper
2 thick slices of good sourdough or soda bread
½ garlic clove

First, cut the tomatoes into small pieces (about 1cm). Throw them into a mixing bowl with the torn basil leaves, a few glugs of olive oil, some salt and a good pinch of pepper. Toss a few times and set aside.

Assuming you got the sourdough, cut the big round loaf in half down the middle. Then turn one of the halves on its end so that the cut surface is face down. Now cut 1½cm slices across the short section of the bread. Take your slices and toast or grill them on both sides. Don't overdo it – you want to get a nice crunchy surface with a little charring but you still want the bread to be moist inside.

Rub one side of the toast a few times with the cut side of the garlic clove while the bread is still nice and hot. The clove will melt into the bread's hot surface. Drizzle with some olive oil.

Lay the bread down and spoon on the tomatoes. Serve immediately while the bread is still warm.

COTECHINO & PICKLED RADICCHIO BRUSCHETTE

The combination of soft, sweet sausage with firm, bitter leaves gives a great expression of the classic 'agrodolce' (sour-sweet) characteristic found in so many Italian dishes. Buy a good cotechino sausage from an Italian deli and follow the instructions on the packet.

For two bruschette:
120g cooked cotechino
1 handful of pickled radicchio, finely sliced – see page 48
Flaky sea salt and black pepper
2 thick slices of sourdough or soda bread
Extra virgin olive oil
½ garlic clove

Once the cotechino is cooked, mash with a fork and combine with thinly sliced pickled radicchio. Season with salt and pepper.

Toast or grill the slices of bread and rub the garlic clove onto one surface of each piece. Drizzle with olive oil. Pile on the cotechino and radicchio mix and serve while still warm.

GOAT'S CHEESE, ROASTED GRAPE & WALNUT BRUSCHETTE

You will find the combination of cheese and fruit in many areas of Italian cooking and with good reason: they work so well together. There is even a proverb about not telling the peasants how sublime this combination is (see page 207).

This bruschetta is a delicious marriage of deep flavours and contrasting textures. It is very easy to make and incredibly impressive when presented and eaten. You should use a mild, soft goat's cheese, such as Italian caprino, and any type of seedless grapes that you like.

For two bruschette:
10 grapes – any seedless variety
1 small handful of picked thyme leaves
Extra virgin olive oil
Flaky sea salt and black pepper
10 walnut halves
2 thick slices of good sourdough or soda bread
½ garlic clove
1 large handful of soft, crumbly goat's cheese
Runny honey

Preheat the oven to 190°C/Gas 5. You need two separate baking trays; one for the grapes and one for the walnuts. Scatter the grapes on one with almost all of the thyme, a little olive oil, salt and pepper. Shake the tray a few times to coat the grapes and place in the oven for 10–15 minutes until they are starting to colour. Shake the walnuts with a little olive oil only and pop those in for just 5–6 minutes. Remove both from the oven and set aside.

Toast or grill the slices of bread so that they are crunchy on the outside but still have a good degree of give when squeezed. Rub one side of each slice a few times with the cut side of the garlic clove. The clove will melt into the bread's hot surface. Drizzle with some olive oil.

Crumble the goat's cheese onto the grilled bread. Add the roasted grapes and walnuts. These should still be nicely warm. Drizzle with a little good quality runny honey. Cut each slice of bruschetta lengthways, scatter over the remaining thyme leaves and serve.

BROAD BEAN, MINT & RICOTTA BRUSCHETTE

This is easily one of the most popular dishes on the summer menu at POLPO. The bright colours are such strong indicators of the flavours that are to follow, but despite the assertiveness of the ingredients, it is still a subtle and delicate combination. Ricotta is readily available from Italian specialists and even in good supermarkets now.

This dish is a joy to prepare. I don't know about you, but podding and skinning broad beans is one of my favourite kitchen pastimes. No, really, it is.

For two bruschette:
1 good handful of podded broad beans
2 tablespoons extra virgin olive oil, plus more for the bread
Zest of 1 lemon and a little juice
10 mint leaves, roughly chopped
Flaky sea salt and black pepper
2 thick slices of sourdough or soda bread
½ garlic clove
3 tablespoons fresh ricotta

Place the broad beans into boiling water for 5 minutes, remove and plunge into cold water, then drain and skin them. Put the beans in a small bowl and dress them in the olive oil, the lemon zest, a little lemon juice and most of the chopped mint. Season with salt and pepper.

Toast or grill the slices of bread so that they are crunchy on the outside but still have a bit of give when squeezed. Rub one side of each slice a few times with the cut side of the garlic clove so that it melts into the bread's hot surface. Drizzle with some olive oil.

Season the fresh ricotta with salt and pepper, to taste, then spread onto the hot, garlicky bread. Top with the broad beans and garnish with the remaining chopped mint.

STRACCHINO, FENNEL SALAMI & FIG BRUSCHETTE

Stracchino, a soft, spreadable cheese that you can find at Italian delis, is a great ingredient here, and on pizzas too (see page 70), because it is mild and consequently perfect for combining with stronger flavours. The salami, finocchiona, is slightly harder to find than other varieties but worth the hassle. It's flavoured with fennel so has a lovely subtle hint of aniseed.

For two bruschette:
2 slices of sourdough or soda bread
½ garlic clove
4 tablespoons stracchino
6 slices of finocchiona
2 juicy figs, quartered
Flaky sea salt and black pepper
Extra virgin olive oil

Grill or toast the bread slices and lightly rub one surface of each piece with the cut side of the garlic clove.

Spread the freshly grilled or toasted bread with stracchino and then loosely fold on top the slices of finocchiona. Place the quartered figs on top and sprinkle over some sea salt, a grind of black pepper and a good drizzle of extra virgin olive oil.

PEPERONATA
& COPPA PANINO

Panini are pretty universal now and appear as standard in sandwich bars the world over. They are such a handy snack, offering heat, texture, crunch, comfort and, most of all, sustenance.

You can use a number of different bread varieties to make a panino. The easiest, and most common, is ciabatta. This is readily available everywhere. We like to take the dome off the top of the ciabatta so that we end up with a more manageable panino that's sleeker and less bready. Stand your ciabatta on its long, narrow side on a chopping board and use a sharp bread knife to remove about 1cm of bread's domed side.

While you're toasting your panino, you need to apply pressure to squash it together. Sandwich shops use a panini press, as do we. Don't worry if you haven't got one, you could squash the sandwich together with a heavy pan on top of a well-oiled griddle pan. Whatever you do, before you grill or toast, drizzle some extra virgin olive oil onto the outside top and bottom of the ciabatta.

I have this particular panino at least once a week when I feel I need something substantial to see me through to lunchtime. It's what Rachel O'Sullivan, one of our chefs, would call 'a happy sandwich'. Peperonata is a sort of stew of sweet peppers, tomatoes and onions, and the one in this recipe is from a jar. It is extensively used in Venetian bàcari and also available in delis and supermarkets. It's incredibly handy to keep in your larder.

For one panino:
½ red onion, thinly sliced
½ garlic clove, thinly sliced
1 tablespoon extra virgin olive oil, plus more for the outside
    of the panino
4 tablespoons peperonata – from a jar is fine (see above)
5 stoned black olives, sliced
1 small handful of capers
2 cherry tomatoes, halved
1 small handful of flat parsley leaves, chopped
1 ciabatta, cut in half lengthways
Mayonnaise
A couple of slices of coppa (cured pork shoulder)
Rocket leaves

Sweat the sliced red onion and garlic in the olive oil on a gentle heat. Then add the peperonata, sliced black olives, capers, tomato halves and parsley. Gently sauté for 5 minutes and then remove from the heat. The mixture should be glossy, thick and beautifully colourful.

Spread the insides of the ciabatta with mayonnaise. Now layer on the soft and juicy pepper mixture, followed by your slices of coppa and some rocket.

Heat up a well-oiled griddle pan or panini press. Drizzle the top and bottom of the panino with olive oil. Toast or press your sandwich until it is golden and crisp on the outside and then cut in half before serving with plenty of napkins.

COTTO & FONTINA PANINO

Cotto is simply cooked ham. Make sure your ham isn't too thick; you want it thinly sliced so that you can layer it up and get all the lovely folds in cross-section when you cut your panino. Fontina is a strongly flavoured cheese from the extreme north-west of Italy that has a delicious pungency when cooked. With the utmost respect to Denmark, please do not use the Danish variety of Fontina that has a red wax rind and is much milder. It's just not the same thing.

For one panino:
1 ciabatta
A good slab of Fontina
Several slices of thinly cut cooked ham (cotto)
Lettuce
Extra virgin olive oil

Cut the ciabatta in half lengthways and grate a generous layer of Fontina on the bottom half. Layer the thinly sliced cooked ham on top. You want the ham layers to have some height because you're going to be squashing them down in a minute. Finish with a layer of lettuce.

Heat up a well-oiled griddle pan or panini press. Drizzle the top and bottom of the panino with olive oil. Press down, grill or toast the panino and then, when crisp and ready, cut in half before serving. You really want to see those ham and cheese strata.

PROSCIUTTO, MOZZARELLA & ROCKET PANINO

Yes, I know. It's a cheese and ham toastie. But this classic combination of prosciutto and stringy, light mozzarella just never gets boring. Add the slightly peppery rocket leaves and here you have a sandwich that is definitely grown-up enough to be enjoyed with a salad and a glass of wine – or for breakfast with a coffee.

Ask your delicatessen to slice the prosciutto as thinly as possible.

For one panino:
1 small handful of grated block mozzarella – the hard, cheap kind
1 ciabatta, sliced lengthways
A couple of thinly sliced pieces of prosciutto
1 handful of rocket leaves
Extra virgin olive oil

Grate some mozzarella onto the bottom half of the ciabatta and lay over the thinly sliced prosciutto. Be generous. Finally put on the rocket leaves. Drizzle a little olive oil onto the rocket and close the sandwich.

Heat up a well-oiled griddle pan or panini press. Drizzle the top and bottom of the panino with olive oil then press and toast. Cut in half at an angle before serving.

COTTO & PICCALILLI TRAMEZZINO

Tramezzini are very particular to Venice and Veneto and pop up in bars, cafés, bàcari and even roadside petrol stations. They are over-filled sandwiches made with cheap white sliced bread, crusts cut off, slices pushed down at the edges and then usually wrapped tightly in cling film. You should use the cheapest, thinnest, whitest sliced bread you can find.

For four halves:
Mayonnaise
4 slices of white bread
Piccalilli
6 slices of cooked ham (cotto)

Spread mayonnaise on all the slices of bread as you would butter. Put a layer of piccalilli, either your own or from a jar, onto each slice. On two bottom slices, layer on your thinly sliced cooked ham, piling it high in the middle to give a lot of height. Put the other slices of bread on top.

Push down the edges of the bread together firmly (you are trying to seal the sides), cut off the crusts and cut once diagonally so that you have two triangles. The cross-section of the tramezzino will reveal the anatomy of your sandwich.

TUNA & EGG TRAMEZZINO

This sandwich may seem absurdly humble in a cookbook but it is a very important tramezzino; you see it in one form or another in virtually every coffee shop and wine bar in Venice. This recipe is based on the version made and served at the Red Caffè in the middle of Campo Santa Margherita (see page 298).

For four halves:
1 × 200g tin of tuna, drained
Several spoonfuls of mayonnaise
½ small red onion, finely diced
1 small handful of flat parsley leaves, chopped
4 slices of white bread
2 hard-boiled eggs

Use your favourite type of tinned tuna and mix with mayonnaise. Add the onion and chopped parsley. Mix thoroughly and spread generously as if you were making normal sandwiches.

For that really authentic effect, place a hard-boiled egg on its side in the centre of each sandwich, push the sides of the bread slices down, cut off the crusts and, with a very sharp knife, divide each sandwich in two, diagonally. You should have a lovely cross-section of a bisected egg in each of the tramezzino halves.

FOCACCIA

This is probably the quintessential Italian bread. Its soft, yielding dough is almost sponge-like in texture and it has such a comforting melt-in-the-mouth quality. I love the tang from the rosemary and sea salt crust. And the great thing about focaccia is that it gets even better when you slice your finished loaf and grill the individual slices to add a little char to the flavour combination.

For one loaf:
25g fresh yeast (or 2 × 7g packets fast-action yeast)
650ml warm water
1kg strong white bread flour
25g fine salt
Extra virgin olive oil
Flaky sea salt
1 good handful of small rosemary sprigs

In a large bowl, mix the fresh or dried yeast into the water and whisk until the yeast is dissolved. Add half of the strong white bread flour and use a hand whisk to beat till smooth. At this stage, your mixture will still be very wet, like a pancake batter. Leave, covered with clingfilm, until it has risen but keep a close eye on the 'tide line'. When the mixture starts to fall again (about 1 hour in a warm kitchen, longer in a cooler one), knead in the other 500g of strong white bread flour and the fine salt. Work everything together until there are no lumps.

Transfer the dough to a warm, oiled, clean bowl and leave it to rise for at least another hour. Your dough will be getting full of itself by now so you need to knock it back and teach it some discipline. Repeat this step (rising and knocking back) twice more only if using fresh yeast. Now your dough is ready to use or it can be covered and refrigerated overnight.

Oil your hands and a greaseproof-paper-lined baking tray. Take the dough and manipulate into a large dome. Place on the tray, smear a generous amount of olive oil over the top, cover in clingfilm and leave to rise in a warm place.

Preheat an oven to 200°C/Gas 6. When the dough has increased in size by one third, remove the clingfilm, oil your hands and lightly press your fingers into the dough so that you leave dimples in the surface. Scatter with sea salt and rosemary, pushing the sprigs into the dough.

Bake the dough in the preheated oven until golden brown (about 1 hour but you should check at 45 minutes). To test the bread's 'doneness', tap it on the bottom – it should sound hollow.

GRISSINI

There are such great quality grissini (breadsticks) available in Italian delicatessens that it is often more convenient to go and buy them rather than make them yourself. You've probably got better things to do. If you have the time, however, they are quite easy and fun to make.

For thirty grissini:
50g unsalted butter
200ml milk
10g fresh yeast (or ¾ × 7g packet fast-action yeast)
380g strong white flour
1 handful of grated Parmesan
10g fine salt

Gently melt the butter in a saucepan and add the milk. Bring the heat right down and add the fresh yeast, if using, dissolving the yeast in the milk mixture.

Mix the flour, dried yeast (if using instead of fresh), Parmesan and salt in a large bowl. Slowly add the milk mixture into the bowl until well combined and then turn out onto a floured surface. Knead until you have consistent, springy, smooth dough. Leave in a warm place to rise for 30 minutes then knead back into shape and refrigerate.

Preheat the oven to 150°C/Gas 2. When the dough is chilled roll it out into thin pencils, put on baking sheets and bake in the oven for 25–30 minutes, or until crispy and golden.

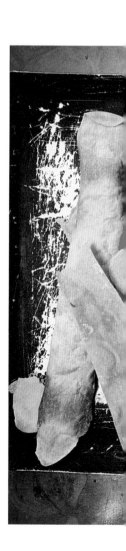

CARTA DI MUSICA

This literally translates as 'music paper' because it's thin and, well, looks like music paper (ish). Again — easy to pick up in a deli but also easy to make. They are great to eat straight out of the oven with a little rosemary-infused olive oil.

For twenty sheets:
300ml water
300g Italian 00 flour
200g fine semolina
Fine salt

Preheat the oven to 200°C/Gas 6. Combine the water with the flour, semolina and a pinch of salt. Knead together into a dough.

Use a pasta machine to roll out 20 thin disks or if you don't have a pasta machine, roll out on a clean, floured surface as thinly as possible. Put onto baking sheets.

Bake in the preheated oven for about 4–5 minutes. Keep an eye on the sheets as they can burn quickly. You want them to be golden yellow and super-crisp.

FISH

Seafood is the lifeblood of Venice. It provides one of the few remaining areas of traditional employment (ie, not connected to tourism) and is an essential part of the distinctive cuisine of the city and the region. If you remove from the equation those heinous trattorie that peddle pizza and lasagne, Venice's remaining real restaurants rely heavily on the daily catch at Rialto. In fact, the genuinely serious fish restaurants don't open on a Sunday and Monday simply because the market does not trade on those days.

It is possible to spend a whole morning wandering from stall to stall marvelling at the vast array at the Rialto fish market. You know with absolute certainty that these beasts were swimming just a few hours earlier. In fact, sometimes the fish are so fresh that they jump up in front of you on the market stalls.

The really interesting produce is the local catch: octopuses, cuttlefish, squid, monkfish, John Dory, clams, pilgrim scallops, sardines, anchovies, most of it from the lagoon. I love the hideous faces of the local monkfish, called coda di rospo, which translates as 'toad's tail'. I adore the inky blackness of the cuttlefish and the tiny tentacles of the baby octopuses, known in Venetian dialect as folpetti, that have only a single row of suckers rather than the double row normally found on tentacles. The local razor clams are so tiny and delicate that they cook in a matter of seconds. The canocie, mantis shrimps that look like trilobites, are fascinating to watch as they clap with their tails. And I always look out for the moéche. These are the tiny soft-shell crabs caught in the lagoon during moulting season. I have tried hard to get these for POLPO but, like a true local delicacy, the natives keep them all for themselves. I can't blame them. They are delicious.

The traditional way of preparing moéche is so intriguing that I will describe it here. This should give you a good idea of what to expect if you ever come across them in Venice. First rinse the live moéche in fresh water. Next, make a nice cold, wet batter from flour, eggs, salt and plenty of Parmesan cheese. Now, drop the live crabs into the cool batter where they spend the most contented 30 minutes consuming as much of the delicious cheesy batter as they can. Meanwhile, you bring a deep-fat fryer to 190°C. Lastly, you take the happy fellows out and drop them in the hot oil for a few minutes until crisp and golden. The shell is soft enough to crush between tongue and roof of mouth and the legs and claws are easy enough to crunch. It's a great dish.

Rather than slavishly giving the ingredients of traditional Venetian fish dishes, many of these recipes have been adapted to use what is available locally. The dish Sardèle in Saór (see page 24), for example, works exceedingly well with any number of oily fish; at POLPO we frequently use sprats or mackerel. Fritto Misto (see page 106) is exactly that, 'mixed fried', so any combination of small fish or shellfish is legitimate, although squid is usually one non-negotiable constituent. Please use as many local ingredients as possible, and don't be too tied to a recipe if the ingredients are out of season.

FRITTO MISTO

POLPO's Fritto Misto has been on the menu since day one and is a very popular dish. The recipe is adapted from that used at Boccadoro, an osteria in the Cannaregio district of Venice. The secret ingredient is the sparkling water that we mix with the egg whites. This makes the batter noticeably light and crisp. The other important detail is to make sure the oil is properly hot — if it isn't around the 190°C mark then the dish can tend towards sogginess.

For four to six:
700g whole squid
12 large raw, shell-on prawns
24 (about 250g) whitebait
3 free-range egg whites
250ml sparkling water
1 litre vegetable oil, for deep-frying
Enough Italian 00 flour to coat the fish
Fine salt
1 lemon, cut into wedges

Wash the squid and pull the tentacles from inside the body. Remove the guts, the gladius, sometimes called the pen (a sort of plastic-like quill that is the creature's internal skeleton) and the ink sac. Cut off the beaky part of the head just above the tentacles. Remove the membrane from the body and cut off the wings. Cut the squid into 1.5–2cm rings, and the wings into the same width. Cut the tentacles into 5cm pieces. Wash the prawns and peel off their shell but leave the head and tail on. Wash the whitebait, leaving them whole. Mix the seafood together carefully in a large bowl.

Lightly whisk the egg whites and sparkling water together. Pour the oil to half fill a deep pan and start to heat it up to 190°C (or until a cube of bread dropped in the oil turns golden in less than a minute). Now, immerse all the seafood, one handful at a time, into the egg white and sparkling water mix. Roll in flour and use a basket or sieve to shake off any excess flour.

Make sure your vegetable oil is very hot and carefully place a handful at a time of the coated seafood in the oil for 30 seconds to 1 minute, or until very lightly golden. Remove with a slotted spoon and drain on kitchen paper. Sprinkle with fine salt and serve with a good wedge of lemon.

MACKEREL TARTARE, HORSERADISH & CARTA DI MUSICA

I am a huge fan of mackerel. It is a plentiful and inexpensive fish with a deep, earthy flavour and a firm, almost meaty texture. I am told it is high in omega-3 fatty acids and vitamin B12, both of which are rather good for you. It is probably my favourite fish and this dish is an incredibly simple but very tasty expression of it. The recipe requires a 5cm ring mould.

Have you ever been mackerel fishing, incidentally? It is an unusual experience. They virtually throw themselves out of the sea and onto your boat – no fishing skill required.

For four:
4 mackerel fillets, skinned
½ cucumber
Fine salt and black pepper
Caster sugar
1 handful of capers and small gherkins, finely chopped
1–2 tablespoons extra virgin olive oil
Juice of 1 lemon
1 handful of flat parsley leaves, chopped
4 sheets of Carta di Musica flatbread – see page 101, or buy from
    a good Italian deli
4 tablespoons horseradish cream – in the recipe for Smoked Salmon,
    Horseradish & Dill Crostini, see page 30

Finely dice the mackerel and set aside. Peel the cucumber, cut it in half lengthwise and scoop out the seeds. Finely dice the flesh, sprinkle with salt and sugar and set aside in a colander for 1 hour to pickle. Rinse and pat dry with kitchen paper.

Combine the mackerel and cucumber with the chopped capers and gherkins in a mixing bowl. Season with salt and pepper, dress with the olive oil and lemon juice and add the chopped parsley. Taste and adjust seasoning if necessary.

Press equal amounts of the mixture into a ring mould on the centre of your four serving plates. Serve with Carta di Musica and a good dollop of horseradish cream.

COD CHEEKS, LENTILS & SALSA VERDE

This is a firm favourite and a dish that, when on the menu at POLPO, sells by word of mouth – we will see adjacent tables telling their neighbours that they must order it. The 'agrodolce' combination of the sweet cheeks and lentils contrasting with the sour salsa verde works beautifully. Your fishmonger will be able to order the cod cheeks for you with a day's notice or so. They are not expensive and have a lovely depth of flavour.

For four to six:
1 large handful of flat parsley leaves
1 handful of mint leaves
1 handful of basil leaves
1 small handful of capers
1 small handful of gherkins
2 tablespoons mustard dressing – in the recipe for Pear,
    Gorgonzola & Chicory Salad, see page 207
Extra virgin olive oil
1kg braised lentils – double the quantity in the recipe for Burrata
    with Lentils, see page 218
1kg cod cheeks, cleaned of any small pieces of bone
Flaky sea salt and black pepper
2 garlic cloves, finely chopped
A good squeeze of lemon juice

First prepare the salsa verde. Make sure you have a very sharp knife and your best heavy chopping board. Finely chop the flat parsley, mint, basil, capers and gherkins. Place all the chopped ingredients in a large bowl and stir in 2 tablespoons of mustard dressing and enough olive oil to make a pourable paste. Leave to one side. Make the braised lentils.

Season the cod cheeks with salt and pepper and pour over some olive oil. Shallow fry the fish in a heavy-based pan for approximately 2 minutes each side, adding the chopped garlic for the last minute and finish with a good squeeze of lemon juice.

Serve the cod cheeks on top of the heated braised lentils and spoon over the salsa verde.

CUTTLEFISH IN ITS INK & GREMOLATA

When POLPO opened, cuttlefish wasn't something you would see on too many menus in London. I suppose the reason they are not used more is because they are ugly, covered in dirty-looking black ink, difficult to clean, not massively versatile and everyone seems to prefer their prettier sister, the squid.

For all these reasons, this is quite a daunting dish. And it is black. I mean, really black. It almost seems to suck light out of the space around it. Someone described a plateful as being as 'black as Darth Vader's helmet.' Another said that it recalled the mud dredged from the bottom of the Venetian lagoon.

But cuttlefish are also delicious and have a thrilling taste of the sea. The addition of the gremolata at the end gives it a lovely fresh zing. This recipe uses the ink from the sac in the centre of the body. Cuttlefish have plenty of ink — or you can buy it in sachets (squid ink is easier to find).

For four to six:
1kg cuttlefish
100ml extra virgin olive oil
2½ garlic cloves
1 large tablespoon cuttlefish or squid ink from a sachet
A large glass of white wine
1 × 400g tin of chopped tomatoes
Salt and black pepper
1 small handful of flat parsley leaves, chopped
Zest of 1 lemon

First clean and prepare the cuttlefish in a sink, retaining the ink sacs. Pull the tentacles from inside the body. Remove the guts and the cuttle bone. Cut off the beaky part of the head just above the tentacles. Remove the membrane from the body and cut off the wings. Cut the body into 1.5–2cm rings, and the wings into 1.5–2cm-long strips. Cut the tentacles into 5cm pieces.

Heat a large pan with enough olive oil to cover the bottom and add 2 whole cloves of garlic. When the garlic is turning brown, remove and discard. Fry the cuttlefish strips over a high heat for 2–3 minutes, or until lightly coloured. Add the cuttlefish ink from the sacs and the extra tablespoon. Add the white wine and the chopped tinned tomatoes.

Now cook the cuttlefish slowly on a low heat for approximately 1½ hours until the cuttlefish is tender but with slight bite and the dish has a thick stew-like consistency, adding a little water if the pan dries out. Check the seasoning.

While the cuttlefish is stewing, you can make the gremolata. Grate the remaining half clove of garlic and combine it with the chopped parsley and lemon zest. Gremolata is a dry, crumbly dressing and so requires no oil or other liquid.

To serve, spoon the gloopy, inky cuttlefish onto pretty white plates for contrast and scatter the gremolata over the top. This dish goes particularly well with polenta (see page 204).

GARLIC & CHILLI PRAWNS

This is such a simple but rewarding recipe that takes no time at all to prepare and even less time to cook. It is one of those dishes that absolutely requires you to use your hands when eating, so remember to place finger bowls and paper napkins on the table. The prawns look so much better with their heads intact and sticking up out of the dish, gazing at the stars.

For four:
21 large shell-on prawns
Extra virgin olive oil
1 hot red chilli, deseeded and finely diced
1 garlic clove, finely diced
A small knob of unsalted butter
Flaky sea salt, if needed

Wash and peel the prawns but leave on the tail and head. This is for presentation and because they are easier to handle.

Heat a few glugs of olive oil in a very large, heavy-based frying pan. Make sure the oil is very hot and then throw in the prawns. Shake the pan a few times. After 1 minute, throw in the chilli and garlic, stir once or twice and remove from the heat. Prawns should not be overcooked, so 1–2 minutes, depending on size, is really all you need. Add the knob of butter.

Each serving will be five prawns so taste the extra prawn to decide whether they need a pinch of salt – often they will not.

BÌGOLI IN SALSA

This was traditionally eaten during Lent when meat was not permitted, but it is now eaten all year round. Bìgoli is simply a long pasta shape like spaghetti and it is only ever served 'in salsa' – in other words, with this sauce and no other. We make our own wholewheat pasta and then push it through a large brass bìgoli press, a bit like those Play-Doh machines you might have had as a child, so that the fat strings ooze from the base: most satisfying.

On the other hand, you could simply use a dried wholegrain spaghetti like all Venetian bàcari do. In fact, recently I had an excellent Bìgoli in Salsa cooked by Francesco, the owner of the tiny All'Arco (see page 310) near Rialto Bridge, and he used standard from-a-packet supermarket spaghetti. Bucatini (a thick hollow spaghetti) is also very good with this sauce.

Serves four to six:
2 large white onions
2 tablespoons extra virgin olive oil
About 20 brown anchovy fillets
A small glass of white wine
300g dried wholegrain spaghetti
A knob of unsalted butter

Finely slice the onions and, in a large heavy-based pan, gently sweat them in the olive oil until so soft that they are nearly falling apart; you are almost melting the onions. Add the anchovies along with the white wine. Cook gently and use the back of a fork to push the fish into the melting onions to create a thick, paste-like sauce.

Meanwhile, cook the pasta in lightly salted water (the sauce is quite salty) until al dente. Drain, retaining just a little of the cooking water, and add the cooked pasta and a knob of butter to the onions and anchovies. Add a little of the retained cooking water – enough to make a sauce that will coat the spaghetti. Mix until combined and serve immediately.

LINGUINE VONGOLE

This dish has taken on something of a legendary status for me. Just saying or hearing those six syllables takes me back to the first time I ever tried linguine vongole.

It was Venice, of course, and it was an over-lit, busy and brash canteen of a place called Ai Quattro Feri, just off Campo San Barnaba. The pasta dishes were only on offer to share — in other words, the minimum order was for two people. I was on my own, but they wouldn't prepare a single portion. I thought I could leave what I wasn't able to eat and ordered the Linguine Vongole for two.

The dish that arrived was huge; a mound of steaming, glistening pasta punctuated with chopped parsley and at least 30 delightful little clams, the whole thing smelling wonderfully of garlic and powerfully of the sea. Of course, there wasn't a scrap left ten minutes later.

For four:
1kg good clams
300g linguine
Extra virgin olive oil
2 teaspoons dried chilli flakes
Flaky sea salt
1 large garlic clove, very finely chopped
250ml white wine
1 large handful of flat parsley leaves, chopped
Crusty bread, to serve

It's all about timing. Get a deep pan of salted water on the boil while you clean the clams by washing them vigorously under cold running water. Scrub if necessary and discard any clams that are cracked or remain open when tapped.

When your water has started to fully boil, place the linguine in carefully and stir slowly once or twice. Add a slug of olive oil to the water and bring down to a gentle boil. Meanwhile, put a very wide frying pan on a medium flame and heat 2 more tablespoons of olive oil.

When the pasta has been boiling for about 3½ minutes, it means it has about 3½ more minutes to go before being perfectly al dente. It is essential that neither the clams nor the pasta overcook. Be very strict with timings. So now throw the clams into the hot oil pan, add the dried chilli, a pinch of salt and the garlic and stir until the clams start to open. This will take no more than 2 minutes. Discard any clams that are still closed. Add the white wine and cover the pan with a lid.

Drain the pasta just retaining a small amount of the cooking water. Quick. Toss the pasta into the clams with the retained cooking water and add the chopped parsley, a few more glugs of olive oil and stir all the ingredients through. Take off the heat and check the seasoning.

Your pan will be a steaming mini masterpiece. Put it onto the table with 4 large shallow bowls, 4 forks, a big bowl to throw the empty shells into, a bottle of chilled Sauvignon Blanc and some crusty bread (ignore what the purists say about never serving bread with pasta – how else are you going to slurp up those lovely juices at the end?). Forget all conversation for the next 10 minutes.

WARM OCTOPUS SALAD

Octopuses* aren't something your fishmonger will necessarily have as a matter of course. You might have to ask him in advance so that he can order one for you. You need just a small beast for this recipe, about the size of a grapefruit.

This recipe is the only instance in this book where you are permitted to use a microwave, and only because it is the technique used by Mirella at Alla Vedova in Cannaregio (see page 306). The version here is based on the dish that she serves at her charming osteria. I love the gentle spice in this salad; it reminds me of the use of smoked paprika in the traditional Spanish preparation of octopus.

For four:
1 medium octopus (1½–2kg)
1 fennel bulb, cut in half
1 onion, cut in half
2 celery stalks, cut roughly
1 handful of parsley stalks, roughly chopped
3 medium waxy potatoes, peeled
1 garlic clove, finely chopped
1 handful of flat parsley leaves, chopped
1 teaspoon chilli flakes
Flaky sea salt and black pepper
4 tablespoons extra virgin olive oil
1 tablespoon lemon juice

First you need to soften up your octopus. You do this simply by freezing it and then thawing; this breaks down the toughness in the cellular structure of the flesh.

In a very large pan, simmer the octopus in unsalted water on a medium-low heat with the fennel, onion, celery and parsley stalks until tender enough to push a fork easily through the flesh. This should take no more than 1 hour. Remove the octopus from the cooking water and allow it to cool. Cut the cooked and cooled octopus into bite-sized pieces, discarding the eyes, beak and the mush inside the head. Remove the skin. Rinse the cut pieces in clean water.

Cut the peeled potatoes into bite-sized pieces, put into a pan of water, bring to the boil and then simmer until cooked. Be careful not to overcook – they should not disintegrate. Drain and set aside.

In a large mixing bowl, gently combine the octopus and potatoes with the garlic, parsley and chilli flakes. Season with salt and pepper and dress with olive oil and lemon juice.

Transfer the dressed octopus to a large serving plate and cover with clingfilm. When you are ready to serve, put the dish in a microwave on full for 30 seconds so that the potatoes and octopus gain a little warmth.

Octopuses is the plural, by the way. Don't let anyone try to convince you that it is octopi. Octopi is a made-up Latin plural that simply does not exist. Octopus is a Greek word, not Latin, so doesn't get one of those Latinate endings like fungus/fungi would. In fact, if you want to be really pedantic about it, the Greek plural would be octopodes.

SOFT-SHELL CRAB
IN PARMESAN BATTER
& FENNEL SALAD

I wrote earlier about the wonderful moéche that inhabit the lagoons of Venice. These are the little chaps that feast on Parmesan and beaten eggs just moments before being plunged into hot oil. Unfortunately, moéche don't travel, so this is the nearest approximation. It is the inside-out version of that delicacy, with the Parmesan batter on the outside.

The little fennel salad that goes with the crab should not be overlooked. Its aniseed flavour and pleasing texture really add to the whole dish.

For four:
3 medium free-range eggs
2 teaspoons bicarbonate of soda
360g Italian 00 flour
50g finely grated Parmesan
Flaky sea salt and black pepper
500ml iced water with a handful of ice cubes
1 bulb of fennel
1 litre of vegetable oil, for deep-frying
4 small soft-shell crabs
4 generous tablespoons mayonnaise

For the batter, whisk the eggs lightly and then add the bicarbonate of soda, most of the flour and the Parmesan. Mix thoroughly and season with salt and pepper. Then slowly add the iced water, whisking gently all the time until the mixture resembles, well, batter I suppose – but not a smooth one: the more lumps and the colder the better.

Use a mandoline or a very sharp knife to cut the fennel into wafer-thin slices and set aside.

Half fill a deep saucepan with the vegetable oil and start heating it up to 190°C (or until a cube of bread dropped in the oil turns golden in less than a minute). Sprinkle a little flour over the crabs and place them in the batter using tongs. Remove and let any excess batter drip off. Place them no more than 2 at a time into the hot oil. Fry until golden brown and crisp (usually about 3 minutes). Drain on kitchen paper.

Place a tablespoonful of mayonnaise on 4 plates, lay on an equal amount of raw shredded fennel onto the dollop and place the soft-shell crabs on top.

BREADED SARDINES WITH CAPER MAYONNAISE

I have vivid memories of being fed sardines as a child. It always felt like something of a punishment; the beasts were tinned, came with a cloying tomato paste and, to make things worse, were known as 'pilchards'. As my palate has matured, I have come to love the sardine and, perversely, now occasionally find myself drawn to the once-terrifying canned fellow, relishing its nostalgic flavour and texture.

This is a very pretty way to serve fresh fillets of the humble sardine, which gives it additional crunch and a bold, zesty flavour.

For four to six:
6 sardines
1 handful of capers, rinsed
4 tablespoons mayonnaise
1 small handful of oregano leaves, chopped
Zest of 1 lemon
200g panko breadcrumbs (available from oriental supermarkets)
Seasoned flour, for coating
2 medium free-range eggs, lightly beaten
Extra virgin olive oil
Lemon wedges, to serve

Ask your fishmonger to top, tail, gut, clean and fillet 6 sardines so that you have 12 fillets: 3 per person or 2 for a lighter dish.

Prepare the caper mayonnaise by chopping the capers roughly and mixing them through the mayonnaise.

Mix the chopped oregano and lemon zest into the panko. Roll the sardine fillets in the seasoned flour and shake off any excess. Then drag them through the beaten egg and lay into the panko breadcrumbs, first on one side and then the other.

Fry the breaded fillets in a large heavy pan with plenty of hot oil until golden brown (about 3 minutes on each side). Drain on kitchen paper and serve with the caper mayonnaise and a wedge of lemon.

WHOLE SEA BREAM

One of my most memorable meals was a simple supper I shared with my wife Jules many years ago in Kefalonia, Greece. Cheap local wine, cool breeze coming off the bay, skin slightly tight from a day in the sun and a simply grilled whole sea bream each. Delicious. This may seem like a small betrayal to Venice but I do occasionally go elsewhere. (And besides, the Ionian islands were ruled by the republic of Venice from 1204 to 1809. Though admittedly I didn't visit until a little while after this.)

Just make sure your fish is fresh: gills red, eyes bright and clear, no fishy smell — simply the salty aroma of the sea.

For two:
2 medium sea bream – about 400g each
Flaky sea salt
Extra virgin olive oil
1 handful of flat parsley leaves, finely chopped
½ garlic clove, finely chopped
1 lemon

Clean the fish by cutting its belly from its head to its bottom. Take everything out and discard. Scale the fish by running the blade of your knife horizontally down the body. Wash the fish inside and out. (Or your fishmonger can do all of this for you.)

Thoroughly dry the fish. In the Mediterranean many people leave their fish in the sun for half an hour before they grill it so that it dries. Our chef Tom saw someone using a hair dryer to achieve the same effect in Croatia! If the fish is too wet this will create steam and cause the fish to stick.

Season the fish with a little salt and olive oil and place on a preheated medium to high heat griddle or barbecue. Don't be tempted to move the fish – just leave it to cook.

The average-sized sea bream, say 400g, will take approximately 6 minutes to cook each side. When you turn the fish, do so gently; you don't want to tear that lovely flesh. To check that the sea bream is done, make a tiny incision through to the spine. You want the fish to be white, not clear, but still moist. Stir the finely chopped parsley leaves and garlic into a little olive oil and drizzle over the skin. Serve with lemon.

In my opinion, there is nothing more satisfying and more delicious than food that is this simple.

WARM SQUID SALAD WITH CAVOLO NERO & CHICKPEAS

Not so long ago, cavolo nero was a rare ingredient outside Italy and could be found only in Italian delicatessens or specialist food halls. Thankfully this rich brassica is now more widely available, even in smart high street supermarkets. It has most in common with Savoy cabbage, and gets its name because of its colour: dark green bordering on black. It is deep in flavour as well as hue and is delicious simply steamed and served with butter, sea salt and freshly ground pepper. Its long fleshy leaves taper down to a short stem and one of the great beauties of cavolo nero is that it doesn't have a heart; it is virtually all leaves.

Serves four to six:
2 heads of cavolo nero
2 large or 3 medium squid (about 1kg)
Extra virgin olive oil
Flaky sea salt and black pepper
3 garlic cloves, finely chopped
1 red chilli, deseeded and finely sliced
5 medium tomatoes, quartered, seeds removed and roughly chopped
1 × 400g tin of chickpeas, drained and rinsed
50ml white wine

Remove the leaves of the cabbage by holding the stem between your thumb and index finger and running the thumb and index finger of your other hand down the stem to pull the leafy part away. It will separate easily. Blanch the leaves in boiling salted water for 2 minutes and refresh in iced water to stop the cooking process. Drain and roughly chop.

Wash the squid and pull the tentacles from inside the body. Remove the guts, the gladius, sometimes called the pen (a sort of plastic-like quill that is the creature's internal skeleton) and the ink sac. Cut off the beaky part of the head just above the tentacles. Remove the membrane from the body and cut off the wings. Cut the body into 1.5–2cm rings, the wings into long 1.5–2cm strips and the tentacles into 8cm pieces.

Pour 3 tablespoons of olive oil into a very hot frying pan, place the squid in, add a little salt and pepper, the chopped garlic and chilli, the chopped tomato flesh, the cavolo nero and the chickpeas. Add a splash of wine and cook on high heat for 1–2 minutes. When the cabbage has started to collapse and the wine has almost bubbled away, remove from the heat. Check the seasoning and serve.

MUSSELS & CLAMS WITH GARLIC BREADCRUMBS

If you fly into Venice in daylight you will often see the lagoon from both sides of the aeroplane. Look closely at the surface of the water and you can spot the many cultivating rows used for mussels. Venetians love their bivalves and use them extensively in a range of seafood dishes, particularly the various versions of Spaghetti ai Frutti di Mare you will find in their restaurants.

Mussels add earthiness and texture, and if you have chosen well you will have the very plump, deeply orange beasts. Clams lend subtlety and sophistication. They also have that thrilling taste of the sea. Breadcrumbs finish this dish well as an effective thickener for the juices but also to add a little crunch.

For four to six:
100g old bread
Extra virgin olive oil
1 small handful of flat parsley leaves, chopped
A large pinch of dried chilli flakes
1 garlic clove, finely chopped
Flaky sea salt and black pepper
1kg mussels
1kg clams
100ml white wine
Bread, to serve

Preheat the oven to 180°C/Gas 4. Make your breadcrumbs first by tearing whatever leftover bread you have into pieces, scattering the bits on a baking tray and pouring a good amount of olive oil over them. Place the tray into the oven for 5 minutes or so, until the bread is crisp and golden. Remove from the oven and set aside.

When cool, place the bread in a food processor with the chopped parsley, half the dried chilli, half the garlic and a little salt and pepper. When the bread has been whizzed into fine crumbs, taste some, adjust the seasoning and add some more olive oil if they are too dry.

Now clean the mussels and clams under cold running water, removing any beards or barnacles with a small knife. It's a good idea to have a little nail brush to help scrub all the mud and sand off the outside of the shells. Discard any that are cracked or that remain open when tapped.

Heat a large pan and add some olive oil. Throw in the mussels and clams with the remaining chilli and garlic and stir until the shells start to open.

As they do so, throw in the white wine and cover the pan with a lid. After 2 minutes all the shells should be open. You must discard any that are not.

Add a handful of the breadcrumbs at this point as these will thicken the sauce and give a fantastic flavour. Spoon into shallow bowls and sprinkle on the remaining crumbs. Serve immediately with bread.

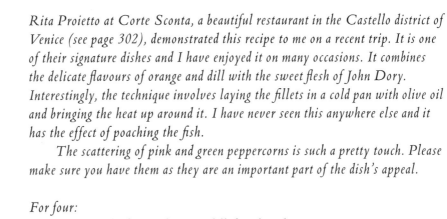

JOHN DORY WITH ORANGE, FINE HERBS & PINK PEPPERCORNS

Rita Proietto at Corte Sconta, a beautiful restaurant in the Castello district of Venice (see page 302), demonstrated this recipe to me on a recent trip. It is one of their signature dishes and I have enjoyed it on many occasions. It combines the delicate flavours of orange and dill with the sweet flesh of John Dory. Interestingly, the technique involves laying the fillets in a cold pan with olive oil and bringing the heat up around it. I have never seen this anywhere else and it has the effect of poaching the fish.

The scattering of pink and green peppercorns is such a pretty touch. Please make sure you have them as they are an important part of the dish's appeal.

For four:
1 large handful of mixed mint, dill, basil and sage
Extra virgin olive oil
4 fillets of John Dory
1 garlic clove, finely sliced
Flaky sea salt and ground black pepper
50ml fish stock
70ml lemon juice
70ml orange juice
1 small handful of pink and green peppercorns
4 slices of orange (optional)

Start by finely chopping the herbs with a very sharp knife. Set them aside.

Drizzle a good glug of olive oil in a large shallow pan for which you have a lid. Carefully lay the four fillets of John Dory skin-side down in the pan and add the garlic with a good pinch of salt and pepper. Scatter the chopped herbs over the fish and place the pan onto a medium flame. When the pan starts to sizzle, add the stock, lemon juice and orange juice and put a lid on the pan.

After no more than 4 minutes, remove the fillets and lay onto 4 warm plates. Turn the heat up fully, add the peppercorns and bubble the juices until they start to reduce (about 2 minutes). Take off the heat and pour the reduced juices onto the John Dory fillets. Garnish each with a slice of orange, if you like.

BRAISED SCALLOPS, PANCETTA & PEAS

Scallops and peas are perfect companions. This recipe brings a little salty contrast to the sweetness of peas and scallops with the addition of pancetta.

In Venice, the scallops are usually the local variety known as 'pilgrims'. They are exquisite and relatively small. If you are using the diver-caught scallops, on sale at most good fishmongers I know, then they will be significantly larger. If they are particularly big, simply slice them in half horizontally.

For four:
8 rashers of thinly sliced pancetta
2 tablespoons extra virgin olive oil
16 spring onions
500g peas – fresh if you can, frozen if not
2 heads of baby gem lettuce, cut into bite-sized pieces
50g unsalted butter
12 small scallops (or 6 sliced in half horizontally if very large)
Crusty bread, to serve

Cut the pancetta into 2cm strips. Fry in a large pan with the olive oil until browned. Cut the spring onions into 5cm pieces and add to the pan. When they have wilted slightly add all the peas and enough water to cover. Simmer for 3 minutes for frozen peas and 5–6 minutes for fresh peas.

Add the chopped baby gem lettuce and the butter and continue to simmer gently. After 1 minute add the scallops and simmer for 1 more minute. Take off the heat and serve almost as a broth in shallow bowls. Have some good crusty bread in the middle of the table to mop up the juices.

PRAWN RISOTTO
WITH MONKSBEARD

*This is a dish that utterly depends on the quality and availability of the
ingredients. Make sure you buy healthy-looking fresh prawns and use them
within a day.*

*Monksbeard, known in Italy as 'barba di frate' or 'agretti', is not easy to
come by. It grows in early spring on marshy areas near the sea and looks like
a bush of unruly chives in its natural habitat and like a scraggly green beard when
picked. A good greengrocer might be able to get hold of it for you or else you could
substitute it with marsh samphire. Monksbeard has a salty, mineral taste and
almost pops when you eat it.*

For four to six:
1kg shell-on prawns
Extra virgin olive oil
2 large onions, 1 roughly chopped and 1 finely chopped
1 garlic clove, finely chopped
1 celery stick, roughly chopped
A pinch of dried chilli flakes
A glass of white wine
1 heaped tablespoon tomato purée
1 litre fish stock
50g butter – at room temperature
400g risotto rice – carnaroli is best
Flaky sea salt and ground black pepper
A glass of dry vermouth
1 small bunch (about 100g) of monksbeard
     (or marsh samphire), trimmed

Carefully pick the shells and heads off the prawns, retaining the shell and
head. Put the peeled prawns to one side and wash them. Meanwhile, heat
a glug of olive oil in a large heavy-based saucepan. Sweat the roughly
chopped onion in the oil with the chopped garlic and celery for 5 minutes.
Add the chilli flakes and all the prawn shells and heads. Keep stirring
until the prawn heads start to stick to the pan and turn dark. Throw in
the glass of white wine and stir in the tomato purée. When the wine has
evaporated, pour in the litre of stock and bring to a gentle boil.

Keep the stock gently bubbling for 30 minutes. Take off the heat and
strain the liquid into a new large saucepan. This is the stock that you now
need to keep simmering and use as you make the risotto.

Using a large heavy-based pan, slowly sauté the finely chopped onion in a
glug of olive oil and 20g of the butter until the onion becomes translucent

and glossy. This will take about 15 minutes on a low heat. Don't let the onions turn brown.

Add the rice, a pinch of salt and a twist of pepper and stir for 2 minutes, coating every grain. Add the glass of vermouth. It will let off a cloud of steam and evaporate quite quickly. Add a large ladleful of the stock and let the rice absorb the liquid, stirring slowly all the time. Add another ladleful to cover the rice and repeat this process. As they absorb the stock, the grains of rice release starch and the whole mixture takes on a lovely creamy consistency.

After 12 minutes or so, taste the rice – it should still have a firm bite and be about 2 minutes away from being perfectly al dente. Add the shelled prawns and the monksbeard. Keep the rice moist with more stock, if necessary, and stir gently. Check that the prawns are nicely pink and take off the heat. Add the remaining butter, stir once, and serve.

MOSCARDINI

This is a dish that brings a smile to people's faces. Moscardini are baby octopuses and are available by special order, usually frozen, from your fishmonger. The tiny cephalopods are terrifying to the squeamish but great fun to the adventurous. They keep their shape and are remarkably animated with their legs twisting in lovely spirals. They have a gentle texture when cooked and really benefit from this powerful marinade as their natural flavour is rather subtle.

This recipe makes a very large batch, perfect for decanting into small dishes with toothpicks for ease of spearing. Children love these little creatures; just remove any large pieces of chilli.

For a large feast or twenty small portions of party food:
1kg moscardini (baby octopuses)
1 litre vegetable stock
300ml olive oil
50ml red wine vinegar
2 teaspoons fennel seeds
1 shallot, very thinly sliced (ideally on a mandoline)
Leaves from 1 small bunch of oregano, roughly chopped
Flaky sea salt and black pepper
2 garlic cloves, very thinly sliced on a mandoline or with a razor blade
1 red chilli, deseeded and finely sliced

Defrost and wash the moscardini. Bring a large pan of vegetable stock to the boil and cook the moscardini in it until tender – usually about 10–12 minutes on a lively simmer. Drain and set aside to cool.

Meanwhile, combine all the other ingredients in a large non-metallic container. Put the cooked moscardini in and make sure they are fully covered. Place into a fridge to marinate for at least 24 hours.

When you serve, make sure each portion has a good array of chillies, fennel seeds, shallot and so on, but not too much oil.

BEET-CURED SALMON

This is such a versatile recipe. Once you have cured your salmon and sliced it thinly, you can layer it on top of crostini, serve it as part of a fish platter or present it with a light salad as a starter. In every case the beautiful deep red colour and the beetroot cure will be a talking point. The simple addition of horseradish improves the flavour and gives a lovely sharp kick.

A really impressive and delicious way to present this is as a cold plate along with the Baccalà Mantecato (page 38), some smoked anchovies (these are available in good delis, particularly Spanish ones), grilled focaccia drizzled with olive oil and a scattering of chopped parsley.

For one side of salmon:
600g salmon fillet
250g raw beetroot
85g flaky sea salt
85g caster sugar
1 bunch of dill, roughly chopped
Zest of 2 oranges
4–6 black peppercorns, crushed
50ml vodka
Horseradish cream, to serve – in the recipe for Smoked Salmon,
    Horseradish & Dill Crostini, see page 30

Remove the skin, blood line and belly fat from the salmon being very careful not to take any flesh away. Peel and grate the beetroot using the large side of a cheese grater. Mix all the ingredients together, except the salmon.

Find a non-metallic container just big enough for the fish. Put the beetroot mixture over and under the salmon to create blanket around it. Place clingfilm over the top and weigh it down with a few small plates.

After 24–36 hours your salmon will have changed colour to an alarming blood red. Excellent! Remove it from its bath, wash off the curing ingredients, pat dry with kitchen paper and then carefully slice as thinly as possible using the biggest, sharpest knife you have.

Use the beet-cured salmon however you like, but remember to add horseradish cream. You can keep the fish in the fridge, wrapped in clingfilm, for about a week, cutting off pieces as wanted.

TUNA CARPACCIO & PINK PEPPERCORNS

The word carpaccio means 'thinly sliced', right? You see it on menus all the time: beef carpaccio, octopus carpaccio, swordfish carpaccio, pineapple carpaccio... Wrong, I'm afraid.

Carpaccio is a dish that was invented in 1950 in Harry's Bar, Venice, and is named after the Venetian Renaissance artist Vittore Carpaccio, celebrated for his vivid use of the colour red in his paintings. It has nothing to do with the thinness of the slices, it is simply because the original dish of fresh raw beef was such a striking hue. However, this is what etymologists call 'a lost cause'. When I mention it now to anyone who will listen, I'm usually told to shut up.

This is another one of those dishes that is more about careful assembly than cooking. The quality of the tuna you buy is paramount. It should be a good thick square block of deep red flesh – it looks more like meat than fish. The garnish includes fennel tops. These are the feathery growths you get on fennel bulbs. You only need the fronds, not the crunchy vegetable underneath. If you have difficulty getting this, fresh dill will work instead.

This is such a pretty and delicate dish in terms of flavours and presentation, and benefits from delicate, feminine crockery.

For four to six:
180ml olive oil
Juice of 2 limes plus the zest of 1
1 red chilli, deseeded and finely sliced
1 garlic clove, very finely sliced on a mandoline or with a razor blade
½ teaspoon caster sugar
Fronds from 1 fennel bulb, finely chopped – retain a few unchopped
    for a garnish (or use dill)
Flaky sea salt and black pepper
300g excellent raw tuna
20–30 pink peppercorns

For the dressing, put the oil, lime juice, lime zest, sliced chilli, sliced garlic, sugar and chopped fennel fronds (or dill) into a clean empty jam jar with a pinch of salt and a grind of pepper. Making sure the jam jar lid is tightly fitting, close firmly and then shake vigorously to combine the ingredients and flavours. The dressing should emulsify slightly. Dip your finger in to taste and add more sugar and salt if necessary. I always do my vigorous shaking over a sink, just in case the lid isn't quite tight enough.

Place the tuna in the freezer for 30 minutes. You don't want it to freeze but it will firm up enough for you to slice it more effectively. Take a very sharp knife and carefully carve slices as thinly as you can from the fish.

Lay as many of the paper-thin slices as you need to cover each of your pretty plates. Give the slices one or two folds for a bit of height, sprinkle over 5 pink peppercorns per person, add the retained fennel top garnishes and dress with a tablespoon or so of the lime dressing per person.

PILGRIM SCALLOPS WITH LEMON & PEPPERMINT

I have been eating at a restaurant called Alle Testiere (see page 302) for about ten years and was lucky enough recently to do a little bit of cooking with the chef Bruno in the tiny kitchen. It really is no more than a cupboard with a window, a sink and a stove. This recipe is for one of their signature dishes. It has only three ingredients, if you discount what you should already have in your larder, and is the epitome of simple cooking.

Pilgrim scallops are known as 'canestrèli' in Venice and are very small, dainty scallops with a subtle, slightly buttery flavour. They can be tricky to find outside Italy, but I have seen them at fish markets, so you might have some joy if you ask your fishmonger in advance. Otherwise, use the smallest scallops you can find; this dish is all about delicacy.

For four to six:
1kg pilgrim (or other small) scallops in the shell
4 tablespoons extra virgin olive oil
1 garlic clove, very finely chopped
Juice of 1½ lemons
12 very small slices of lemon
20 leaves of mint – peppermint is traditional
Flaky sea salt and black pepper

You must make sure the scallops are clean and free from grit, sand, mud and dirt. Open them with a small sharp knife and clean inside and outside under cold running water.

Into a pan put the olive oil, garlic, lemon juice, lemon slices and mint leaves. Place the scallops shell-down into the pan. Sprinkle over some salt and grind over some pepper.

Put the pan on a moderate heat until the oil starts to get hot. Cover and leave for 4–5 minutes on a low to medium heat.

Remove the scallops and place them face-up on your plates. Scatter over the lemon slices, if you like. Reduce the lemon and mint sauce over a high flame for a few moments and then spoon this over the scallops.

Serve immediately, perhaps with a simple soft leaf salad.

MEAT

There is something eerie but compelling about Venice in the winter. Maybe it is the lack of tourists or the echoes of Donald Sutherland and Julie Christie in *Don't Look Now*, running along narrow calle in a deserted city. Perhaps it has something to do with the often-freezing temperatures and icy winds that are absorbed into the stone and marble around you and into your very bones. After dark, the city becomes even stiller and emptier so that if you take a wrong turn and find yourself in an unfamiliar alleyway or courtyard, you can get seriously spooked. You hear only the hollow sound of your own footsteps on the hard stone and the gentle lapping of water against the canal walls. The streetlamps reflect in the rippled surfaces of the rio like ghosts and the church bells do little to reassure.

As you wander around Venice on these frozen winter days, you will frequently happen upon a campo or a campiello. These vary in size but almost always have a large circular well at the centre. They are paved now, of course, but in previous centuries they were grassy pastures (campo means field) where cows would graze – an image that is difficult to reconcile now with a city that seems to be carved from marble.

Winter is the time of the year when meat takes on most relevance in Venetian cooking. The warming stews and one-pot dishes found in rural Veneto become popular in the city, and you will also notice that the restaurants become more innovative. The sure-fire tourist trade is thinner on the ground and chefs tend to be more imaginative. The comforting winter dishes of Venetian-style calf's liver, sòpa coàda (a pigeon and bread soup made in the oven) and soprèssa (garlic sausage) are just what you want to find on a menu and, even if you can't see them listed, always ask. My favourite of the lot, and you will come across this even in small bàcari, is muséto, a pork sausage made mostly with meat from the head of the pig. It is steamed and then kept hot in a broth until it is served, usually with potatoes and lentils.

There are a few butchers around the Rialto Market and in the residential districts, away from the couture boutiques and trinket shops selling Murano glass clowns. And these are wonderful places, packed with produce and colour, selling cured meats, smoked hams, sausages and salted cuts. But also you will catch glimpses of whole muntjacs, rows of skinned rabbits hanging by their feet, delicate-looking game birds and beautifully butchered and presented lamb racks. The great frustration being a visitor is that one doesn't always have a kitchen to use to take advantage of the produce.

Horse is a favoured meat here too – in fact there is a horse specialist in Rialto by the market – Macelleria Equina – where you will find meat that is so lean and so intensely red that you wonder why it can't be got more readily in other countries. I have also eaten braised donkey with peppercorns and polenta in the foothills of the Dolomites in Friuli. This dish has yet to make it onto the menu at POLPO.

FEGATO ALLA VENEZIANA

This dish of calf's liver with melted onions and sage is so closely associated with Venice that I knew we had to get the recipe just right. I had such an idealized version in mind that whenever I tried it in any number of restaurants, it always fell short of my expectations. It was back in London that our head chef Tom nailed it with the following iteration.

The key is the balance of sweetness and the texture of the onions. The onions really are very important here. You want the large white Spanish onions you find in most supermarkets or, if you are very lucky, the smaller white Italian cipolle you get in specialist markets and some department store food halls. They are sweeter and more delicate than regular cooking onions. When cooked, they need to be so soft that they almost dissolve.

This is a comforting classic that is best when accompanied by polenta (see page 204).

For four to six:
6 tablespoons extra virgin olive oil
2 large white onions, finely sliced
Flaky sea salt and black pepper
12 sage leaves
1kg calf's liver, trimmed, cleaned and thinly sliced
50ml white wine
50g unsalted butter

Pour 2 tablespoons of the olive oil into a heavy-based pan and sweat the onions with a pinch of salt on a very low heat for approximately 30 minutes, or until very soft. The onions will become translucent and should not burn – they should be only lightly brown. Add a grind of pepper. Take off the heat and set aside.

Cut the sliced liver into thin triangles. In another large heavy-based pan, heat the remaining 4 tablespoons of olive oil on a medium flame with the sage leaves and when hot add the liver, season, and cook until brown on both sides (if your pan is hot this should be no more than 1 minute in total). Add the melted onions, heat through, and add the wine. Turn up the heat to get it bubbling for 1 minute and then immediately add the butter, simmer for another minute, check the seasoning and serve.

BASIC TOMATO SAUCE

There was a time when Italian restaurants in London and New York tended to offer a very narrow version of Italian cooking. Often the menu would consist of a variety of pasta dishes with a small range of sauces, nearly all of them tomato-based. We have moved on from this simplistic notion of Italian cuisine but I still have a respectful admiration for the old-school approach of the traditional trattoria where tomato sauce is king. I also love the way New Yorkers refer to these places as 'red sauce joints'.

A good tomato sauce is such a useful commodity to have to hand and, although the convenience of tinned passata has made shortcuts incredibly tempting, I would still recommend that you make a big batch of this sauce and save what you don't use in the fridge. It will keep for up to a week. (In Italy it keeps longer — you simply scrape the mould off the top before using.)

For one and a half litres:
100ml extra virgin olive oil
1 onion, finely sliced
1 garlic clove, chopped
Scant ½ tablespoon fine salt
¾ teaspoon black pepper
Small pinch of chilli flakes
750g fresh tomatoes, quartered
3 × 400g tins of chopped tomatoes
1 small handful of oregano, chopped
Caster sugar, if necessary

Heat half the oil in a saucepan on a medium-low flame and in it sweat the onion, garlic, salt, pepper and chilli for 15 minutes. When the onions are glossy and transparent, add the fresh tomatoes and the rest of the oil and cook gently for a further 15 minutes.

Add the tinned tomatoes, bring to a gentle bubble and then simmer on a very low heat for 1 hour.

Take the pan off the heat and add the chopped oregano. You can season the sauce with a little sugar, to taste — it will depend on how sweet your tomatoes are. Transfer to a food blender or use a hand-blender to blitz for a few minutes. If you like, pass through a fine sieve.

PORK & BEEF POLPETTE

Who doesn't like meatballs? A good meatball is a sublime thing. It has texture and flavour and it's comforting and fun. We often think of it as an American invention. For as long as I can remember, New York has been in the grip of a meatball craze, a sort of revival of the working-class, Depression-era staple that is cheap, easy to make, nutritious and tasty. You can, after all, pretty much mince anything as long as you flavour it with enough salt, pepper and herbs. But meatballs are, of course, as Italian as spaghetti. In Italy they call them polpette.

Talking of spaghetti, you could serve these meatballs with any pasta but they go particularly well with linguine. Just make sure you are generous with the tomato sauce and grate plenty of Parmesan over your individual servings.

We make and serve 25,000 polpette* a year at POLPO. The classic pork and beef is our most popular variety.

For thirty balls (three to five per person):
1kg minced pork
500g minced beef
3 medium free-range eggs
Scant ½ tablespoon fine salt
1 teaspoon black pepper
150g breadcrumbs
Small pinch of dried chilli flakes
3 garlic cloves, finely chopped
½ handful of flat parsley leaves, chopped
1½ litres tomato sauce – see page 149

Preheat the oven to 220°C/Gas 7. Combine all the ingredients (except the tomato sauce), massage thoroughly and roll into 45g spheres, like large golf balls. Place the balls on a greased baking tray and roast in the oven for 10 minutes, turning once, until they are starting to brown. Then poach in the tomato sauce in a covered saucepan for 10 minutes.

Serve 3–5 balls per person with some lightly toasted focaccia to mop up the juices.

* A word on Italian vocabulary. Our second restaurant was called Polpetto. Many people have informed me that it means meatball. Not so. A polpetta is a meatball, the plural being polpette because it is feminine. Polpetto is a rather cutesy word, not often used, that is a diminutive for baby octopus. The plural here would be polpetti because it is masculine. You will rarely see this in restaurants as Italians generally call small octopuses moscardini. I hope that's all clear now...

SPICY PORK
& FENNEL POLPETTE

Fennel is such a versatile vegetable and we use it in a number of dishes. But you can get the flavour of fennel without having to use the bulbs. This recipe uses fennel seeds, which marry so well with the ground pork and chilli that this meatball has become my favourite of all the varieties we make.

For thirty balls (three to five per person):
1.5kg minced pork
3 medium free-range eggs
150g breadcrumbs
Large pinch of dried chilli flakes
20g fennel seeds, lightly toasted and ground in a pestle and mortar
Scant ½ tablespoon fine salt
1 teaspoon ground black pepper
1.5 litres tomato sauce – see page 149

Preheat the oven to 220°C/Gas 8. Put the pork, eggs, breadcrumbs, chilli flakes, ground fennel seeds, salt and pepper into a large mixing bowl and massage thoroughly. Roll into 45g balls and place them on a greased baking tray and roast in the preheated oven for 10 minutes, turning once, until they are starting to brown.

Then poach the meatballs in the tomato sauce in a saucepan for 10 minutes. Serve 3–5 balls with some sauce and hunks of lightly toasted focaccia.

LAMB & PISTACHIO POLPETTE

Lamb and pistachio is a classic Middle-Eastern combination but one that has found its way into adventurous kitchens in other parts of the world too. Lamb lends itself well to mincing and I particularly like the contrasting textures in this meatball. The five-spice is perhaps a surprising ingredient in an Italian dish but it is subtle, aromatic and helps to pull the flavours together.

For thirty balls (three to five per person):
125g shelled pistachio nuts
2 tablespoons extra virgin olive oil
1 onion, finely diced
2 garlic cloves, finely chopped
Scant ½ tablespoon fine salt
Large pinch of five-spice powder
1.5kg minced lamb
1 large free-range egg
150g breadcrumbs
1 teaspoon ground black pepper
Extra virgin olive oil
1.5 litres of tomato sauce – see page 149

Preheat the oven to 170°C/Gas 3. Roast the pistachio nuts on a baking sheet for 10–12 minutes, or until lightly brown – take care they do not burn. Leave to cool slightly then roughly chop.

Heat the olive oil in a large pan and in it sweat the onion, garlic and a pinch of the salt. Sauté on a low heat, adding the five-spice powder. When soft and translucent, allow to cool. You can either leave this as a rough mixture or purée it in a small food processor.

Turn the oven up to 220°C/Gas 7. In a large bowl, combine the lamb, egg, breadcrumbs and chopped pistachio nuts and work together with your fingers. Now add the rest of the salt, the pepper and the onion mixture and massage thoroughly. Roll into 45g balls, place them on a greased baking tray and roast in the oven for 10 minutes, turning once, until they are starting to brown. Then poach in tomato sauce for 10 minutes.

Serve 3–5 balls with a few spoonfuls of the tomato sauce and some soft bread such as focaccia.

DUCK & PORCINI
POLPETTE

There is such depth of flavour and intensity in these wintery meatballs that they are better suited to serving as appetizers. They work very well individually as canapés with a little sauce over each and a toothpick skewer for picking them up. Duck legs and porcini are easy to come by, and confit legs increasingly so. I can buy them in large glass jars at my local supermarket, usually suspended in pearly white duck fat. I have also seen them at farmers' markets, and department store food halls will usually stock them.

For thirty balls (three to five per person):
80g dried porcini
4 duck legs, skin removed
1 confit duck leg, skin removed
Extra virgin olive oil
1 onion, chopped
1 carrot, chopped
1 celery stick, chopped
1 small handful of parsley stalks, chopped
A glass of red wine
60g breadcrumbs
1 × 400g tin of chopped tomatoes
Fine salt and black pepper

Submerge the dried porcini in enough warm water just to cover, and leave for 20 minutes. Drain and set aside, reserving the liquid. Remove the flesh from the bones of both the fresh and confit duck. Put the meat in the fridge and brown the bones in a large heavy pan with a little oil. Add the onion, carrot, celery and parsley stalks and sweat for 5 minutes. Add the red wine and reduce by half. Add the porcini liquid and 2 litres of water. Let this simmer gently for 1 hour. Allow to cool, strain into a large jug and set aside.

Preheat the oven to 220°C/Gas 8. Take your duck (both raw and confit) and grind through a medium grinder, or pulse in a food processor. Finely chop the drained porcini and put in a mixing bowl. Add the breadcrumbs and the ground-up meat and season generously. Roll into small balls and place on a greased baking tray. Roast in the preheated oven for 10 minutes, turning once, until they start to brown.

In a very large saucepan place the balls, the tin of tomatoes and half the porcini duck stock. Simmer gently for 1½ hours or until the balls are soft and tender. Remove from the heat and serve with a little sauce.

PORK BELLY, RADICCHIO & HAZELNUTS

This dish has become something of a signature at POLPO. Whenever we take it off the menu to add some seasonal variety or to trial a new dish, there is an outcry from regulars. It is a simple recipe with only three main ingredients. The sweet, hot cooking juices from the pork coat and wilt the bitter radicchio leaves, and the hazelnuts add a good crunch. A compelling combination.

For four to six:
200g hazelnuts
1 onion, thickly sliced
1kg pork belly
Flaky sea salt and black pepper
Extra virgin olive oil
1 large head of radicchio
1 tablespoon red wine vinegar

Preheat the oven to 180°C/Gas 4 and roast the hazelnuts on a baking sheet for 5 minutes, taking care they do not burn. Leave to cool then roughly chop.

Turn the oven up to 240°C/Gas 9. Put the sliced onion into a roasting tin and place the pork belly on top, skin-side up. While the oven comes up to temperature, score the skin of the pork with a very sharp knife or a razor blade. You could use a clean Stanley knife from your toolbox. Rub salt into the skin and smear with a little oil. Place the pork in the preheated oven for 10–15 minutes, until browned.

Turn the oven down to 160°C/Gas 3 and continue to cook for about 1 hour or until tender. During the cooking time add a little water if the pork and onions start sticking or burning. Remove the pork belly when cooked and allow to rest and cool slightly. Collect all juices from the pan and pass through a fine sieve.

Core the radicchio and remove all the leaves, tearing the larger ones in half. Place in a large mixing bowl. Use the warm pork fat and juices to dress the radicchio salad with the toasted and chopped hazelnuts.

Slice the pork belly and place in the bowl with the radicchio and hazelnuts. Splash over the red wine vinegar and add a pinch of salt and pepper. Scrunch the salad together with your hands so that the dressing mixes through and the radicchio warms and wilts.

COTECHINO, LENTILS & MOSTARDA

Cotechino Modena is a fresh sausage made from pork, back-fat and pork rind. I have heard it described as trotter sausage so it would be fair to assume that there is a reasonable amount of pigs' trotters in the mix too. You could buy the ingredients, sausage machine and skins and have a go at making it yourself, but I would strongly recommend you pop to your nearest good Italian deli and buy some ready-made.

Cotechino is traditionally served at Christmas and New Year with lentils, or mashed potatoes and cabbage, and a sharp condiment to cut through the fattiness of the sausage. At POLPO we serve the sausage with lentils and mostarda (mustard fruits). Again, you could go through the lengthy process of making mostarda yourself, or visit your local Italian deli and pick some up. It comes in a small jar and looks like jam.

For six:
1 large cotechino sausage
400g Puy lentils
3 tablespoons extra virgin olive oil
2 large carrots, finely chopped
3 celery sticks, finely chopped
1 small onion, finely chopped
3 garlic cloves, finely chopped
Leaves from 5 thyme sprigs
Flaky sea salt and black pepper
1 handful of flat parsley leaves, chopped
1 tablespoon Dijon mustard
Small jar of mustard fruits

To cook the cotechino, follow the instructions on the packet – which will usually include boiling the sausage in its plastic wrapping for approximately 30 minutes.

Meanwhile, cook the lentils in enough water to cover them by 5cm. Don't add salt at this stage as this will toughen the lentils. When they are cooked but still holding a small bite (about 20–30 minutes), drain and rinse in cold water.

As the cotechino and lentils are cooking, heat the oil in a large pan and sweat the chopped vegetables and garlic with the thyme leaves, a large pinch of salt and a grind of black pepper.

When the vegetables are softened, add the cooked lentils and a splash of water to stop them sticking to the bottom of the pan. Peel the cooked sausage and slice into 1cm rounds.

To finish the dish, mix the chopped parsley and mustard into the lentils, check the seasoning and spoon into a large warm shallow bowl. Place the sliced cotechino on top of the lentils and serve a generous spoonful of the mustard fruits on the side.

RABBIT, SAGE & APRICOT TERRINE

Venetians love rabbit. Northern parts of Veneto were well known for wild rabbit and hare and you still see them displayed in butcher shops all over the region, skinned and hung up by their hind legs. The wild beasts are quite rare now but farmed rabbit is common and has a very pleasant, slightly milder taste.

The classic Venetian rabbit recipe is Coniglio alla Veneta – a simple but delicious stew. I really like the use of the meat here, with apricots and sage – a light and aromatic combination – as a terrine. It's versatile and tasty and keeps in the fridge for several days.

For twelve:
1 whole skinned rabbit, with offal
1 onion, quartered
2 carrots, halved
2 celery sticks, halved
1 small handful of black peppercorns
100ml Marsala
Flaky sea salt
2 tablespoons extra virgin olive oil
1 large shallot, roughly chopped
1 garlic clove, finely chopped
Leaves from 1 bunch of sage, finely chopped
150g dried apricots, finely chopped
25g leaf gelatine
Crispy toast, frisée and cornichons, to serve

Put a 2-litre terrine mould (or loaf tin) in the freezer to chill. Remove the offal from the skinned rabbit and set aside. Put the rabbit in a very large pot with plenty of salted water. Add the onion, carrot, celery and peppercorns. Bring the rabbit to a hard boil, skim off any scum that floats to the top and reduce the water to a good simmer.

Continue to simmer the rabbit until it is tender (approximately 30–40 minutes). When it is cooked, remove from the water and allow to cool. Strain the cooking liquid and reduce down to 1 litre, adding 50ml of the Marsala towards the end. Check that the stock is very well seasoned and almost bordering on overly salted. Set the stock aside.

While the rabbit is cooking you can prepare the offal. You need only the heart, the liver and the two tiny kidneys. Discard the lungs and roughly chop everything else.

In a pan heat the olive oil and in it sweat the shallot, garlic and half the sage. When the shallots become translucent add the prepared offal and cook for about 5 minutes. Add the remaining Marsala and boil for a couple of minutes. Put this mix in a food processor and pulse until you have a coarse paste. Tip this into a bowl and mix in the apricots and the rest of the sage.

Take the cooled cooked rabbit and pick the meat off the bones then roughly chop into 1cm dice. Combine the chopped meat with the apricot and offal mix and check the seasoning; the mix needs to be well seasoned as it will be served cold.

Soften the gelatine leaves in ice-cold water, gently squeeze out the water and stir into the warm rabbit and Marsala stock. Take the terrine mould or loaf tin out of the freezer. Place the rabbit mix into it and pour over the liquid, making sure it gets in and around all the pieces of meat and around the edge, tapping the mould or tin firmly on the work surface. Cover the terrine with clingfilm and carefully place it in a roasting dish half full of chilled water. You want to chill the dish as quickly as possible then put the terrine in the fridge overnight to set.

When you want to serve the terrine, place it briefly in a bath of hot water. Put a plate on top of the mould and quickly turn it upside-down to release the terrine. Serve slices with thin crispy toasts, frisée and cornichons.

HAM HOCK
& PARSLEY TERRINE

This is a classic combination and a really handy terrine to serve as a simple appetizer. It keeps for a week in the fridge without deteriorating but you must not serve it too cold. It needs to be brought up to room temperature for the lovely salty flavours to express themselves.

Ham hocks are the knuckle part of the pig's leg nearest the trotter and have a distinctive nutty flavour and firm texture. If your butcher doesn't have them he can order them for you for the following day.

For about twelve:
2 ham hocks
1 onion, quartered
1 carrot, halved
1 celery stick, halved
1 small handful of whole black peppercorns
1 bunch of flat parsley, leaves separated from stalks
1 shallot, finely diced
35ml red wine vinegar
2 tablespoons Dijon mustard
1 tablespoon wholegrain mustard
Black pepper
25ml port
25g leaf gelatine
Crispy toast, to serve

Put a 2-litre terrine mould or loaf tin in the freezer. Put the ham hocks in a large pot with plenty of water, the onion, carrot, celery, peppercorns and parsley stalks. Bring to the boil then turn down the heat and simmer, skimming off any scum that rises to the surface. Partially cover the pot.

The ham hocks will take approximately 1½ hours to cook, depending on their size. The best way to check is to insert a long, thin knife right into the centre of the meat. If you can remove the knife without any resistance from the meat then it is cooked. Remove the ham hocks from the water and allow to cool. Sieve and reserve the cooking liquid.

Meanwhile, in a small mixing bowl place the diced shallot and mix with the red wine vinegar and the mustard. Leave to stand for 1 hour.

When the hocks are cool enough to handle, take the meat off the bone and discard any fat or gristle. Cut the meat into 1cm cubes. Combine the meat with the shallot and mustard mixture. Roughly chop the parsley leaves and work them into the mixture. Add a good twist of black pepper. Transfer the cooking liquid to a large saucepan and bring to the boil. Before it gets too hot, give it a taste. It needs to be very well seasoned. Adjust if necessary and add the port. Boil for 2 minutes.

Take 400ml of this liquid and keep the rest for general use later (it makes a great pea and ham soup). Place the gelatine leaves in iced water until soft. Squeeze out the water and dissolve the gelatine leaves in the warm ham stock.

Take the terrine or loaf tin out of the freezer and in it place the meat mixture. Pour the liquid over the top, making sure it gets in and around all the pieces of meat and around the terrine mould, tapping the terrine dish on the work surface to help this along. Cover the terrine with clingfilm and cool quickly by putting it in a roasting tin half full of cold water. Refrigerate the terrine overnight to set.

Bring the terrine to room temperature and very briefly place in a bath of hot water. Put a plate on top of the mould and turn it upside-down to release the terrine. Serve the terrine in slices with crispy toast. It also goes very well with chopped boiled eggs mixed with mustard and mayonnaise.

DUCK, BLACK OLIVE & TOMATO RAGÙ

There is a meat restaurant in Venice called La Bitta. The owner, Debora, takes its mission very seriously; 'No Fish' she declares proudly on the menus and business cards. This dish was inspired by something very similar that our head chef Tom and I had there. I remember we had a bottle of Amarone della Valpolicella, too, and it was a worthy companion.

Duck legs are the tastiest part of the bird and have a deep, smoky flavour. This dish doesn't suffer from shyness and the combination of tomatoes and black olives helps the duck deliver intensity and gaminess. You can eat this on its own but is goes very well with polenta or potato gnocchi.

For four to six:
300g cherry tomatoes, halved
Flaky sea salt and black pepper
Extra virgin olive oil
5 duck legs
1.5 litres tomato sauce – see page 149
1 large handful of good-quality black olives, stoned
1 large handful of green peppercorns
Black pepper
1 small handful of flat parsley leaves, chopped, to serve
Polenta or Gnocchi, to serve – see page 204 or 194

Preheat the oven to 180°C/Gas 4. Season the halved cherry tomatoes. Shake on a few splashes of olive oil and place on a baking tray in the oven. Roast them until they blister and almost collapse (about 25–30 minutes). Remove and set aside.

Preheat the oven to 240°C/Gas 9. Take the duck legs, season, and roast until the skin is brown and crisp (about 10 minutes). Reduce the heat to 200°C/Gas 6 and continue to roast until the meat is tender (about 1 hour). Set aside and strain the cooking juices for use later.

By now, the duck legs will have cooled and you can pick the meat off the bone. Roughly chop the larger pieces and leave the smaller ones.

Put the tomato sauce in a large pan on a medium heat, add the olives, peppercorns, some ground pepper and about 150ml of the duck's roasting juices. Bring the sauce to a medium simmer for 30 minutes or so, until it is very thick and has no trace of water in it. Add the duck meat and continue cooking for 10 minutes. Just before you take the pan off the heat, add the oven-roasted tomatoes and a little parsley. Stir and serve.

FLANK STEAK WITH PORTOBELLO MUSHROOMS

This is among the most popular dishes at POLPO and another one with very few ingredients. I love its simplicity. The cut of beef here is flank steak (called fianco in Italian). It is often confused with skirt, but flank comes from the section of the cow further back from the chest plate. It is a very flavoursome cut but can be tough if too rare or if overcooked. You must try to get your meat cooked perfectly 'medium' so that there is still a lot of pinkness to the flesh and just a little blood when cut.

Portobello mushrooms are widely available but any large flat mushroom will do. The finished dish is almost like a warm steak salad and is a delicious and hearty meal for a sunny autumn day.

For four:
800g flank steak – 5cm thick
Flaky sea salt and black pepper
Extra virgin olive oil
4 handfuls of rocket leaves
8 large Portobello mushrooms, sliced
2 garlic cloves, very finely chopped
1 small handful of flat parsley leaves, chopped

Generously season the outside of the meat and, using a hot, oiled griddle pan, grill the steak on both sides until it is cooked to your liking, but certainly no more than medium (about 10–12 minutes in total). Leave it to rest somewhere warm for 15 minutes.

Meanwhile, dress the washed rocket leaves in a few splashes of olive oil and a pinch of salt and a grind of pepper. Place the rocket on each of your serving plates.

In a frying pan, fry the sliced mushrooms in 2 tablespoons of olive oil with the chopped garlic and most of the chopped parsley. When soft and shiny, remove from the heat and set aside.

Your meat will be well rested so place it onto a firm chopping board and thinly slice. Lay the juicy pink slices on top of the rocket, scatter the mushrooms evenly and serve with a little drizzle of oil and the remaining parsley.

OSSO BUCO WITH SAFFRON RISOTTO

Osso buco means 'bone hole' – not particularly appetizing as a description but very accurate; there is a bone in the middle with a hole in it. If you're very lucky, you get a big wobbly piece of marrow to suck out at the end of your feast. It is by no means Venetian and originates from the region of Lombardy, but since it is a dish with such wide appeal, it appears all over Italy.

For six:
Extra virgin olive oil
6 pieces of veal shin on the bone – about 4cm thick, hind-leg is best
Seasoned flour, for coating
3 carrots, finely chopped
3 celery sticks, finely chopped
2 large onions, finely chopped
Leaves from 2 sprigs of rosemary, roughly chopped
Leaves from 4 sprigs of thyme
2 garlic cloves, finely chopped
Flaky sea salt and ground black pepper
A glass of white wine
2 × 400g tins chopped tomatoes
40g unsalted butter
2 litres vegetable stock
300g risotto rice – carnaroli is best
A glass of dry vermouth
Good pinch of saffron
1 handful of grated Parmesan

Preheat your oven to 180°C/Gas 4. In a large heavy-based pan heat a couple of glugs of olive oil until hot. Cover the veal shins with enough seasoned flour to coat. Fry them in the oil until nice and brown on both flat sides. Remove and set aside.

Pour a glug of olive oil into a separate heavy-based pan and add the chopped carrots, celery and one of the onions. Sweat these slowly and add the chopped rosemary, thyme leaves, garlic and a good pinch of salt and grind of pepper. When the vegetables are starting to stick add the glass of white wine and allow to bubble away for 2 minutes, scraping all the good bits off the bottom of the pan. Add the chopped tomatoes and a cup of water and bring to the boil. Now, transfer everything to a large roasting tray with the browned meat. Make sure all of it is covered with the tomato mix and cover with foil. Place in the preheated oven for around 2 hours, or until meat is almost falling off the bone.

When there are about 30 minutes to go with the veal shins, you should make the risotto. Put a glug of oil and half the butter in a saucepan and in it slowly sauté the other chopped onion until it becomes translucent and glossy. This will take about 15 minutes on a low heat. Meanwhile heat up the vegetable stock in another saucepan.

Add the rice to the onion and stir for 2 minutes, coating every grain. Add the glass of vermouth. This will create a large cloud of steam and a wonderful smell as it evaporates. Add a large ladle of the hot stock and let the rice absorb the liquid, stirring all the while. At this point, delicately scatter the pinch of saffron into the rice. Add another ladle to cover the rice and repeat this process as the rice absorbs the stock and the grains release their starch and the whole mixture takes on a delightful creamy consistency. After 15 minutes or so, taste the rice – it should be creamy but still have a slight bite.

When the rice is done, remove from the heat and carefully fold in the Parmesan and the remaining butter. Cover and let the whole thing rest for a few minutes.

Take the veal from the oven and remove the foil. The meat should be practically falling off the bone. Serve the risotto onto each of the 6 plates and place a veal shin on top of each mound of yellow rice. Spoon the sauce onto the meat and serve.

170

PIGEON SALTIMBOCCA

A classic saltimbocca, which translates as 'jump in the mouth', is made with veal. This is a variation that uses one of my favourite birds, pigeon. It's effectively a red meat with a serious, almost smoky taste, particularly when cooked medium-rare. They are farmed as squab but if you are lucky enough to get wild wood pigeon the breasts are plumper and the flavour deeper.

Pigeon breasts are fairly small so this recipe requires 2 per person. They really must be placed on a bed of polenta to serve.

For four:
8 pigeon breasts
1 garlic clove, very finely chopped
Black pepper
8 sage leaves
8 very thin slices of prosciutto
Extra virgin olive oil
A glass of red wine
A good knob of butter
Wet polenta, to serve – see page 204

Clean the pigeon breasts of any blood and gunshot, remove the skin and sprinkle each with a little chopped garlic and some freshly ground black pepper. Place a leaf of sage over each breast and carefully wrap in prosciutto.

Put a good frying pan (non-stick if you have one) onto a medium flame with a little olive oil. When it's hot carefully place each pigeon breast into the pan, presentation-side down. When nice and brown (about 3 minutes), turn over and brown the other side too. After no more than 2 minutes, turn off the heat. Remove the breasts from the pan and set aside somewhere warm to rest for 10 minutes.

To make the sauce, bring the juices in the pan back up to a bubble and add the glass of red wine and the knob of butter. Stir for a minute or so and then remove from the heat.

Serve the rested pigeon breasts on a bed of wet polenta and spoon over the juices from your pan.

BRAISED OX CHEEKS

Ox cheek is one of those intensely tasty cuts that butchers rarely promote. I'm not sure why, as it is the perfect slow-cook stewing meat. It is now easier to get hold of, however, and your butcher will always be able to order it for the next day.

I enjoy this way of preparing it as all the vegetables and herbs are used for the marinade and then discarded. You are left with the ox cheeks and little else, but the flavours of the earlier ingredients are very evident.

For ten to twelve:
2kg ox cheeks
A glass of red wine, for the marinade, plus another for the sauce
1 head of garlic, cut in half
1 carrot, roughly chopped
2 celery sticks, roughly chopped
1 onion, roughly chopped
3 sprigs of rosemary
3 juniper berries
2 bay leaves
Zest of 2 oranges
1 litre meat stock
1 × 400g tin of chopped tomatoes
75g seasoned flour
Extra virgin olive oil
30 cherry tomatoes, halved
30 green olives, stoned and halved
1 handful of flat parsley leaves, chopped
Wet polenta, to serve – see page 204

Trim the ox cheeks of any excess fat or sinew and discard. Put the trimmed meat in a large non-metallic container. Add the red wine, garlic, carrot, celery, onion, rosemary, juniper berries and bay leaves. Make sure the meat is nicely coated in the mixture you have prepared and then cover and place in a fridge for 24 hours to marinate.

Next day, take the container out of the fridge, remove the meat and set aside in the fridge, covered. Transfer the marinating liquid and vegetables to a large heavy-based pan and put on a high heat. Bring the contents of the pan to a high bubble and add the orange zest. Now pour in the meat stock along with the tin of tomatoes, bring to the boil then turn down and simmer, covered, for 1 hour. Take the pan off the heat, allow it to cool, and then strain the liquid through a large sieve. Set the stock aside.

Preheat the oven to 160°C/Gas 3. Liberally dust the meat in seasoned flour and shake off any excess. Heat a few splashes of olive oil over a high flame in a large heavy-based casserole dish and place the floured meat in carefully, making sure the meat is brown all over. Set the meat aside briefly while you add the other glass of wine. It will bubble and you will be able to scrape the bottom of the pan with a wooden spoon to lift the sticky residue and create a little sauce that will thicken the end dish.

Put the meat back in the casserole dish and pour the stock onto it. Cover and place in the preheated oven for 2½ hours, or until the meat is tender. Meanwhile, lay the cherry tomatoes on a baking tray, sprinkle with salt and olive oil and roast in the oven for the final 30 minutes.

Portion or slice the meat onto individual plates, and top with the blistered tomatoes, olives and parsley. Serve with a generous dollop of wet polenta.

BOLLITO MISTO

Boiled meat doesn't get a good press. Perhaps it's the association with dreadful school meals and grey meat. This dish is as far away from that as it is possible to get. It is delicious: light, delicate, gently salty and sticky, and full of flavour.

The clear broth that accompanies the meats is worth the price of admission alone. I could happily drink this and nothing else.

For six:

1 ox tongue
4 carrots
4 celery sticks
1 large onion, quartered
½ bunch of parsley stalks
10 whole peppercorns
Flaky sea salt
6 new potatoes
3 free-range chicken breasts, skinned
1 × 200g cotechino sausage
2 large handfuls of flat parsley leaves
1 handful of mint leaves
1 handful of basil leaves
1 small handful of capers
1 small handful of gherkins
2 tablespoons mustard dressing – in the recipe for Pear,
    Gorgonzola & Chicory Salad, see page 207
Extra virgin olive oil

Ideally, start this recipe the day before you want to eat the dish. In a heavy-based pan, place the ox tongue in enough water to cover it by 5cm, with 2 of the carrots (quartered), 2 sticks of the celery (quartered), the onion, parsley stalks, whole peppercorns and a good pinch of salt. Simmer for 2 hours, or until easily pierced with a carving fork. Remove the tongue and allow it to cool slightly before peeling and placing in the fridge, covered.

Strain the liquid into a clean pan and use it to poach the chicken breasts. Cut the remaining carrots and celery sticks at an angle, cut the potatoes in half and put them all in the pan with the chicken. These will all take about 10–15 minutes to cook at a simmer. Remove the chicken and vegetables and set aside in the fridge, covered. Strain the liquid again and also set it aside in the fridge.

Cook the cotechino as per instructions on packet. Leave to cool. Put in the fridge, covered.

It is best to leave everything overnight. This way you can remove any fat that has gathered on the surface of the broth.

You should prepare the salsa verde on the day you want to eat the dish. Make sure you have a very sharp knife and your best heavy chopping board. Finely chop all but a small handful of the flat parsley, the mint, basil, capers and gherkins. Place all the chopped ingredients in a large bowl and stir in 2 tablespoons of mustard dressing and enough olive oil to make a pourable paste.

To serve, slice the tongue, cotechino and chicken, and reheat in the meat broth with the potatoes and the vegetables. You must heat the broth and the contents gently. Delicately ladle the broth, meats and vegetables into elegant shallow bowls. Finish with a scattering of roughly chopped parsley leaves and a tablespoon of salsa verde.

CHICKEN COTOLETTA

Italian chicken recipes are a relative rarity, surprisingly so — perhaps it is because Italians prefer their chickens to produce eggs. You tend to see more guinea fowl than chicken on Italian restaurant menus.

No matter. This is an easy and refreshing way to serve chicken breast and has the added advantage of being quicker to cook because of the flattened meat. The breadcrumbs add texture and provide a pleasing crunch. Serve these cutlets with a simply dressed salad of baby gem lettuce or frisée and a dollop of mayonnaise for a great light lunch.

For four:
2 free-range chicken breasts
Flaky sea salt and black pepper
Juice of ½ lemon
1 handful of Italian 00 flour
3 medium free-range eggs, lightly beaten
About 300g panko breadcrumbs (available from oriental supermarkets)
Extra virgin olive oil

Slice the chicken breast lengthways with your knife parallel to the board. Place each piece between sheets of clingfilm. Use a rolling pin or saucepan to flatten the breasts so that they end up just slightly fatter than a pound coin. Season and sprinkle with the lemon juice.

Get 3 separate plates ready, 1 with flour, 1 with the lightly beaten eggs and 1 with the breadcrumbs. Dip both sides of the flattened chicken into the flour, shake off any excess, then dip gently into the egg and finally into the breadcrumbs.

Heat a pan with plenty of oil and fry the chicken until golden brown.

RABBIT CACCIATORE

The name of this dish comes from the Italian word for hunter. I have also seen 'cacciatore' translated as 'hunter-style'. It's a romantic notion that this dish may have been prepared by the burly hunter-gatherer who shot the bunnies in the first place.

It's a great, hearty stew of a dish and one that requires relatively little preparation before you throw it in the oven for half the afternoon.

For six to eight:
1 rabbit, cut into 13 pieces (ask your butcher to do this)
Seasoned flour
Extra virgin olive oil
3 carrots, finely chopped
3 celery sticks, finely chopped
1 large onion, finely chopped
2 garlic cloves, finely chopped
Leaves from 2 rosemary sprigs, roughly chopped
Leaves from 4 thyme sprigs
Flaky sea salt and black pepper
A glass of white wine
2×400g tins chopped tomatoes
1 handful of black olives, stoned
1 handful of flat parsley leaves, chopped

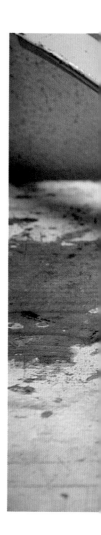

Preheat the oven to 160°C/Gas 3. Put the rabbit pieces into a plastic bag with enough seasoned flour to coat. Give it a good shake and remove the meat pieces. In a large heavy-based pan heat 150ml olive oil until hot. Fry the floured rabbit pieces in the oil until they are nicely browned on all sides. Remove and place to one side.

Add the chopped carrot, celery, onion and garlic to the pan with the roughly chopped rosemary leaves and thyme. Season with salt and pepper. Turn down to a medium flame and soften for 5 minutes or so.

When the vegetables are starting to stick, add the glass of white wine and allow it to bubble away for 2 minutes, scraping all the good bits off the bottom of the pan. Add the chopped tomatoes, a cup of water and the black olives, then bring to the boil. Add the browned meat, again bring to the boil, cover and place in the preheated oven for around 1½ hours or until meat is almost falling off the bone.

Taste the sauce and adjust seasoning if necessary. Serve in large bowls and finish with some roughly chopped parsley. This dish goes particularly well with buttery mashed potato or hunter-style, with crusty bread.

LAMB CHUMP
WITH CAPONATA

Chump is the cut between loin and leg and is one of the most flavoursome parts of the lamb. It is inexpensive and easy to cook but not as well known as other parts of the animal. The marinade is a lovely way of imparting an aromatic nuance to the meat without having to use the garlic and rosemary at the cooking stage. When grilling the lamb, please make sure the griddle is very hot indeed — you want to get a lovely charring to the flesh. And, as with all lamb, it can be difficult to cut if too rare, so aim for a nicely pink 'medium' inside.

The Caponata recipe is on page 246 and should be served at room temperature, not hot like a soup.

For four:
4 lamb chump chops
Leaves from 1 large handful of rosemary, finely chopped
2 garlic cloves, finely sliced
Extra virgin olive oil
Flaky sea salt and black pepper
4 portions of Caponata, to serve — see page 246

Remove the skin and any excess fat from your lamb chumps. Lay them in a large container and scatter over all the chopped rosemary and the sliced garlic. Pour over enough olive oil to coat the meat, turn a few times, cover and marinate overnight in the fridge.

The next day, remove the chops and brush off the rosemary and garlic. Season each piece of meat with salt and pepper. Using a very hot griddle pan, grill for approximately 6 minutes on each side or until the lamb has a good colour on the outside but is still pink on the inside. Let the meat rest for 5 minutes and then thinly slice and lay on top of the Caponata.

PROSCIUTTO & BUTTERNUT SQUASH WITH RICOTTA SALATA

This recipe is so simple it is almost embarrassing, but it is one of my favourite uses of butternut squash. When squash is roasted it takes on a remarkably sweet flavour and a delightful velvety texture. And when combined with the salty tang of the ricotta and prosciutto, this dish really sings. It is important that you buy your sliced prosciutto from a good Italian delicatessen. The slices should be so thin that you can almost see through them. You will also get your ricotta salata here — it's a salted, firm variation of the normally soft cheese and is perfect for grating.

For four to six:
2 medium butternut squash
Extra virgin olive oil
Flaky sea salt and black pepper
10 sage leaves, torn
8 large slices of prosciutto
200g ricotta salata
1 handful of pumpkin seeds

Preheat the oven to 200°C/Gas 6. Cut the squashes in half and remove the seeds and the hard stalk. Now cut the remaining halves into large bite-sized pieces. Scatter them onto a roasting tray and splash on a good amount of olive oil, add a good pinch of salt and pepper and the torn sage leaves.

Roast the squash in the preheated oven, until cooked throughout (about 20–30 minutes). A good way to check is to see if a knife can be pushed into the middle and pulled out with minimum force and resistance.

Remove the squash from the oven and whilst still warm put on plates, drape over the thinly sliced prosciutto, grate over the ricotta salata and drizzle with a little olive oil. Sprinkle over the pumpkin seeds for texture and a little added crunch.

WARM DUCK SALAD WITH WET WALNUTS & BEETS

Now I'm going to make things really easy for you here. I have cooked duck legs in their own fat several times to make the classic confit duck leg. Then I discovered that most French food markets, some farmers' markets and department store food halls sell them pre-cooked. Brilliant. They come in jars, suspended in white duck fat and are delicious.

Wet walnuts are one of those great delicacies of autumn and have a distinctive soft bite to them. They are so satisfying alongside the duck and beetroot. And if you are lucky enough to have intact leaves on the beets, reserve them, washed, for the salad.

For four to six:
4 medium beetroots, and their leaves, if available
Splash of red wine vinegar
1 tablespoon caster sugar
2 confit duck legs
1 garlic clove, finely chopped
100g rocket leaves
2 red chicories, divided into leaves
1 tablespoon mustard dressing – in the recipe for Pear,
      Gorgonzola & Chicory Salad, see page 207
1 shallot, finely sliced
100g shelled wet walnuts

First, cook the beetroots in plenty of water with the red wine vinegar and caster sugar. Cook at a gentle boil for 45 minutes or so, depending on their size. You should be able to push a knife through easily when they are done. Remove from the water and allow to cool slightly but peel them while they are still warm. Cut the beets into quarters.

Preheat the oven to 200°C/Gas 6. Take the confit duck legs, remove and discard the skin. Now pick the meat from the legs and place it into a roasting tray. Discard the bones. Add the beetroot and garlic and place in the oven for no more than 5 minutes – just to heat it through.

Put the rocket, beet leaves (if using) and chicory into a large mixing bowl. Add the mustard dressing, the finely sliced shallot, wet walnuts and finally the warm duck and beetroot. Turn a few times to coat everything nicely and then serve.

BRESAOLA, CELERIAC, RADISH & PARSLEY

It has to be said that celeriac is a fairly ugly vegetable: a pale, gnarled and pitted root. It is related, unsurprisingly, to celery, and shares the same distinctive flavour. In its raw state, celeriac has a good crunchy texture and takes on a certain delicacy when grated. In this recipe it acts as a foil to the smoky intensity of the bresaola. I love the little peppery hit from the perky radishes too. This is a lively dish, perfect for a light lunch.

The bresaola must be thinly sliced, so ask at your delicatessen for the lowest setting on a slicing machine.

For four to six:
12 large, very thin slices of bresaola
1 celeriac
Flaky sea salt and black pepper
Caster sugar
8 breakfast radishes, thinly sliced
1 large handful of flat parsley leaves, roughly chopped
Extra virgin olive oil

Lay the bresaola onto plates, folding the thin sheets so that you create a bit of height and texture. You can set this aside while you make the salad.

Take the celeriac and peel the dull outer layer to reveal its bright flesh. Using the large gauge on a cheese grater, grate the celeriac into a mixing bowl along with a pinch of salt and a pinch of sugar. Leave for 30 minutes and then rinse, pat dry and put back in the bowl.

Add the sliced breakfast radishes to the celeriac and the chopped parsley. Splash with a little olive oil and turn a few times in the bowl to coat everything. Carefully place the salad on top of the bresaola and give each plate a twist of pepper.

COLD MEAT PLATE

The cold meat plate on POLPO's menu was inspired by the lovely platter served at La Cantina in Cannaregio (see page 306). I recently visited the owner, Francesco, and worked side by side with him as we prepared one together. It is simplicity itself, assembly rather than cooking, but so deliciously fresh, flavoursome and as pretty as a picture.

Since it is unlikely that you will have a slicing machine at home, ask your delicatessen to slice the meats for you. I recommend you get the slices as thin as possible.

For one large platter (for two hungry people or four lightweights):
10 small, sweet tomatoes – a variety such as Sundream works well
Flaky sea salt
1 × 125g ball of buffalo mozzarella
4 slices of prosciutto di Parma
4 slices of bresaola
4 slices of cured pork shoulder (coppa)
4 slices of good cooked ham (cotto)
5 basil leaves
Extra virgin olive oil
2 teaspoons wholegrain mustard
Good bread, to serve

Make sure all the ingredients have been taken out of the fridge 30 minutes before you start preparing them.

Cut your tomatoes in half, salt them lightly and place in a bowl. Set aside. Tear up the mozzarella into bite-sized pieces.

On a very large plate or platter, lay the slices of meat, making sure there are folds for height and texture. You want this to look beautiful but not too 'prepared'. Leave space in the centre for the mozzarella, the tomatoes and the dollop of mustard.

Put the mozzarella on the plate then finish the tomatoes by tearing in the basil leaves, giving one or two good glugs of olive oil and turning over with your hand. Place on the plate in a pile and then add the mustard in a little mound on its own. Serve with good bread.

OX TONGUE WITH BALSAMIC VINEGAR

These terrifying organs take a bit of getting used to when you are handling them. I'm not usually squeamish about anything in the kitchen – brains, hearts, lungs, testicles… I barely bat an eyelid. But there is something slightly disconcerting about a huge ox tongue because it looks so much like, well, a tongue, I suppose.

You must be brave. Despite its scary appearance, tongue is delicious and has such a satisfyingly firm texture. It goes particularly well with sweet balsamic vinegar – make sure you use a very good quality one with a bit of age.

For four to six:
1 ox tongue
1 carrot, quartered
1 onion, quartered
1 celery stick, quartered
1 handful of parsley stalks
6 black peppercorns
Flaky sea salt
3 medium free-range eggs
100g white flour
250g panko breadcrumbs (you can buy these in oriental supermarkets)
1 litre vegetable oil, for deep-frying
300g endive
Extra virgin olive oil
Very good aged balsamic vinegar

Place the ox tongue in a large pan – you need it to be big enough so the tongue can be fully submerged. Fill with enough cold water to cover the tongue, bring to the boil and add the quartered vegetables, parsley stalks, peppercorns and a large pinch of salt.

Simmer for about 1–1½ hours, or until tender. Remove from the heat and take the tongue out of the pan but don't throw away the cooking water. When cool enough to handle, peel the skin off the tongue. Then pop it back into the cooking liquid until you are ready to use it.

Whisk the eggs and place in a shallow bowl. Set up separate bowls for the flour and the panko breadcrumbs, too. Now remove the tongue from the liquid and cut it into ½cm slices.

Half fill a deep pan with the vegetable oil and bring it up to 190°C (or until a cube of bread dropped in the oil turns golden in less than a minute). Dip each piece of tongue into the flour first, shaking the excess off, then the egg, then the panko crumbs. Finally drop the breaded slices into the hot oil for a few minutes until they have turned golden brown and are hot throughout. Drain on kitchen paper.

Prepare your salad by simply putting the endive into a large mixing bowl with a few glugs of olive oil and a pinch of salt. Turn the leaves a few times with your hand and then place onto your plates.

Lay the slices of fried, breaded tongue onto the plated salad and drizzle with a little balsamic vinegar.

VEGETABLES

Vegetables obey the seasons in a way that meat and fish simply do not. There is a rhythm to what grows, and when it appears in the markets, throughout the year. The hearty greens, brassicas, cabbages and roots of winter give way to the abundance of flowering vegetables and vibrant colours in the spring. Late spring is all about artichokes in Italy; if you ever find yourself in Venice in May, you will see these wonderful green globes absolutely everywhere. Summer is dominated by tomatoes; those amazing buttons of sunshine that have so many delicious manifestations. Autumn brings deep golden hues, reds, ochres and browns. We are spoilt for choice between varieties of pumpkins, mushrooms and marrows.

Nowhere is this changing palette of the seasons more evident than at Rialto Market. You can almost hear the stalls groan under the weight of produce and when you glance down the narrow calle that run into the market like tributaries, you will see many crates of back-up produce, waiting in the wings to replenish the traders' shelves.

But the one vegetable I associate with Venice and Veneto more than any other is radicchio. This striking red member of the chicory family is the pride of the region, particularly the small flower-like variety known locally as Treviso, or more specifically Treviso Tardivo. The leaves grow upwards from the stem and then curl inwards slightly, giving them the appearance of octopuses in retreat. They are magnificent plants, fleshy and bitter when eaten raw but juicy and almost meaty when roasted. Strictly speaking a winter vegetable, I have seen them in the market as early as October and as late as May.

When cooking vegetables, don't be afraid to keep things utterly simple. What, after all, could be more delicious than a handful of asparagus spears plunged into boiling water for a few minutes, drained and served hot with butter and salt? Or that Tardivo radicchio washed, dried, cut into bite-sized pieces, tossed in olive oil and salt and served as a salad?

A useful tip in the preparation of vegetables is blanching. This is the swift boiling of vegetables to the point of tenderness, after which the cooking process is stopped abruptly. Your greens can be reserved for use later (for example, they can simply be heated through just before serving), and it is a very effective way to retain their nutrients, colour and taste. Get a large pan of well-salted water on the stove. Next to this have a large pot of freezing-cold water full of ice. Get ready a set of tongs or a sieve. When the water is boiling rapidly throw in your vegetables. Do not add too many vegetables at once; if the temperature of the water rapidly drops you have added too many. When your vegetables are just tender, remove them from the water and plunge them into the iced water. When they have cooled fully, remove from the water, drain and put to one side for when you need them. It's a great trick and one well worth getting into the habit of doing as a matter of course.

CAVOLO NERO, GNOCCHI & PECORINO ROMANO

For an Italian restaurant, POLPO doesn't have much pasta on the menu. There are several reasons for this. Firstly, I think that there is so much that is more interesting about northern Italian cooking. Secondly, pasta is rarely offered in Venetian bàcari – they are usually too small to have traditional cooking facilities. Thirdly, in London many of the Italian restaurants are what New Yorkers affectionately call 'red sauce joints', offering a choice of pasta varieties with a choice of sauces. I didn't want POLPO to compete with those places. So, with some very important exceptions such as Linguine Vongole (see page 118), there is very little pasta.

Gnocchi, however, are something else. These little starch bombs are so pleasurable and comforting, we had to put them on the menu. The sauce that goes with the gnocchi in this recipe is one I have been making for years for my family. It is simple, delicious and startlingly green.

For four to six:
500g white potatoes (Maris Piper or similar general-purpose potato)
1 medium free-range egg
About 130g Italian 00 flour (depending on the potatoes used you
    may need more or less)
2 heads of cavolo nero
2 garlic cloves, chopped
1 handful of grated Parmesan
Flaky sea salt and black pepper
2–3 good glugs of extra virgin olive oil
Pecorino, to serve

First make the gnocchi. Boil the potatoes until just cooked, drain and when cool enough to handle pull the skin off and leave them to cool completely. (Cooking them in their skins keeps in more of the flavour.) When the potatoes are cold, grate finely.

Add the egg to the grated potato and about the same volume of flour as the potato – it should be around 130g but could be more or less. Now knead the mixture into a dough – you are looking for it to become one coherent mix with nothing sticking to the work surface. Roll the dough into long 1cm-thick sausages and then cut at 1cm intervals.

To use the gnocchi immediately, you simply cook them in boiling salted water, remove them when they rise to the top and throw them straight in to your chosen sauce.

To use the gnocchi later, place them in boiling water until they bob to the surface, remove and put on a large tray with enough olive oil to coat – this stops them from sticking to each other – and cover the tray with clingfilm. Put in the fridge until needed then simply put the gnocchi into boiling water for 30 seconds before transferring to your sauce.

For the sauce, take the cavolo nero and pull the leaves off the woody stems. Blanch till tender – about 4 minutes – and refresh in cold water, retaining some of the cooking liquid.

Roughly chop the leaves and place in a food processor with the chopped garlic, grated Parmesan, a pinch of salt and pepper and the extra virgin olive oil (use more or less according to how rich you'd like the sauce to be). Blitz, and slowly add some cooking liquid until you have a thick sauce consistency.

Heat the sauce in a pan, adding a little more water if it sticks and throw in the cooked gnocchi and heat through. Scatter some shaved Pecorino over the top and serve.

INSALATA CAPRESE

The intense, grassy, peppery pungency of tomato plants is one of the smells I most associate with high summer. Quite often I will eat a ripe tomato like an apple, but always with a few flakes of sea salt. There are so many things to do with this most flexible ingredient in any kitchen. At POLPO, we sometimes oven-dry them and serve them with a whole buffalo mozzarella, olive oil and oregano, a dish known as Mozzarella Pizzaiola (see page 217). My favourite way to eat tomatoes, however, is as part of an Insalata Caprese.

As is often the case, preparation time and quality of ingredients are directly related – the shorter the first, the better the second must be. Preparation time is about 5 minutes, therefore the quality of the ingredients is everything.

This salad is so easy to make that if you really wanted to show off you could buy the ingredients, take them to a picnic with a mixing bowl, cutting board and knife, and impress your friends by making it in front of them.

For four to six:
20 ripe tomatoes (from your garden, heritage, Datterini
    or San Marzano, or mixed varieties)
Flaky sea salt
4 tablespoons extra virgin olive oil
4 × 125g balls of buffalo mozzarella
16 basil leaves
Good bread, such as Pugliese or focaccia

Make sure your ingredients are at room temperature. If they are fridge cold you must wait 20 minutes for them to de-chill. Cut the tomatoes in half, put them into a large bowl and crunch some salt onto them. Leave for a few minutes to allow the salt to pull on the juices then add half the olive oil and turn twice, gently, with a spoon.

Tear the mozzarella balls into sixths and place onto 4–6 wide shallow bowls. Spoon the tomatoes onto the bowls equally. Tear the basil leaves and throw onto the tomatoes. Dress with the remaining olive oil.

I cannot think of a more heavenly combination of flavours. The bread comes in pretty handy to mop up the milky tomato and olive oil juices at the end. If you're not eating bread, then drink the juices, for goodness sake.

Repeat throughout the summer.

PANZANELLA

Panzanella is a summer peasant salad in which an abundance of tomatoes is mixed with stale bread. Its origins are firmly in Tuscany and it is traditionally made with the dark country bread found in that beautiful region. If the bread is really hard and stale, it is sometimes soaked in water first. I've never done that because my bread never hangs around long enough to go that stale. About a day old is just right.

I have seen this salad prepared so many different ways, with the addition of roasted peppers, capers, celery, anchovies... Hold on, I say. You don't want or need your panzanella to be that complicated. Keep things simple. Resist the temptation to tinker.

For four to six:
About 120g old bread – sourdough is perfect
Extra virgin olive oil
1 large red onion
Flaky sea salt and black pepper
About 20 tomatoes of various sizes
Red wine vinegar
1 large handful of basil

Start by preparing your 'stale' bread. Preheat the oven to 140°C/Gas 1. Take some leftover (but not too hard) bread and tear into 2cm square pieces. Massage some olive oil into the bread and place in the low oven until golden but not too crisp. Set aside.

Finely slice the red onion, put in a bowl and sprinkle with a little salt, then leave for 10 minutes. This will remove any bitterness from the onion.

Make sure you have a good selection of ripe tomatoes at room temperature. Cut them into bite-sized wedges and place in a mixing bowl. Drizzle with a generous amount of good quality extra virgin olive oil, a few glugs of red wine vinegar and season with salt and pepper. Tear up the basil leaves and scatter them into the salad.

Now add your pieces of bread and turn over a few times. Leave in the bowl for 10 minutes and then serve.

ZUCCHINI, BASIL
& PARMESAN SALAD

A startlingly simple salad that is delightful and surprising, this is one of the most requested recipes at POLPO. The trick here is to slice the zucchini as thinly as possible. The wafer-thin slices take on a delicacy that we don't normally associate with zucchini. It is also important to make sure the salad is not overdressed – you want the elements to be daintily and lightly coated rather than doused.

For four to six:
Juice of 1 lemon
6 tablespoons extra virgin olive oil
2 heaped tablespoons finely grated Parmesan
Flaky sea salt and black pepper
4 zucchini
1 large handful of rocket leaves
1 small handful of basil leaves

First make the dressing by mixing the lemon juice with the olive oil, Parmesan and a little salt and pepper.

Finely slice the zucchini on an angle (or use a mandoline if you have one) and put into a bowl. Mix this with the rocket, basil and enough of the dressing to coat. Taste, adjust the seasoning and serve immediately.

VEGETABLES

ROAST POTATOES
& ROSEMARY

Potatoes don't really feature in Italian cooking in the way they do in other European countries. You find potatoes in Italian recipes as an ingredient rather than something to accompany protein – polenta has taken on that mantle.

I did find a recipe for Venetian-style Potatoes, which was simply chopped onions and small-cut potatoes sautéed in butter and olive oil over medium heat for 30 minutes with chopped parsley thrown in at the end. It's actually rather nice.

The recipe below, also using potatoes cut into small, bite-sized pieces, is not a typical Venetian dish, but I like it a lot because it is relatively fast to prepare, very tasty, and great to snack on.

For four to six:
2kg general-purpose potatoes (eg Maris Piper, Estima, Desiree)
1 large handful of rosemary sprigs, leaves picked
Extra virgin olive oil
Flaky sea salt and black pepper

Peel and cut the potatoes into small chunks. Boil in salted water until they are cooked through but holding their shape. Drain in a colander. Shake the potatoes around in the colander until the sides are rough and fluffy. Leave for 10 minutes to cool slightly and lose their excess moisture.

While the potatoes are drying, preheat your oven to 220°C/Gas 7. Heat your roasting tray in the hot oven with about three-quarters of the rosemary, several good glugs of olive oil, salt and pepper. Take the tray out, place your parboiled potatoes in and coat well with the oil and rosemary. Roast the potatoes, turning and shaking every 15 minutes until ready. They should take no more than about 45 minutes.

POLENTA

*Perhaps I ought to take a moment to describe polenta for the uninitiated.
It's a sort of savoury porridge, a bit like semolina, that can be served as a gloop
or set, sliced and grilled. It doesn't sound particularly appetizing, does it?*

*Polenta is made from maize, probably brought from the New World
or possibly by way of Turkey (maize is sometimes called 'gran turco' –
Turkish grain). It was for centuries the cheapest form of sustenance available
to peasants in Italy and became a staple of the poor, leading to many well-
documented periods of disease and nutritional deficiency; they ate polenta
and not much else.*

*These days, it is a comforting and versatile accompaniment, a delicious
substitute for potatoes or bread when eating protein. This dish almost demands
to be served with Fegato alla Veneziana (see page 146), Cuttlefish in its Ink
(see page 112) and Duck, Black Olive and Tomato Ragù (see page 165).
You could do the traditional thing and pour the stiff polenta onto a wooden
board and place it in the centre of the table for everyone to help themselves.*

*Maize polenta is usually yellow in colour. You buy it in Italian
delicatessens and most supermarkets. (Or you could use a variety of the easy-
cook stuff known as polenta svelta. Yes, I know it's cheating, but every osteria
and bàcaro that I know in Venice uses instant polenta so why shouldn't you?
Follow the instructions on the packet.)*

For four to six:
2 tablespoons flaky sea salt
300g polenta
1 handful of finely grated or shaved Parmesan, for wet polenta
A knob of unsalted butter for wet polenta, or extra virgin olive oil
     for grilled polenta

Bring 2 litres of water and the salt to the boil in a heavy-based pan.
With one hand, stir the water clockwise and with the other take handfuls
of polenta grains and let them fall through your fingers a little at a time
whilst stirring continually, always clockwise. Do not change direction.
This is the only way to avoid lumps and ensure a smooth and
consistent result.

Once all the polenta is in the water, reduce the heat and continue to
stir slowly, making sure none of the mixture sticks to the bottom or
sides of the pan. Continue this for 40 minutes until the polenta pulls
away from the sides of your pan. It's really straightforward but time-
consuming and boring.

For wet polenta, finish the dish with a handful of shaved or grated
Parmesan, a knob of butter and a grinding of black pepper.

For grilled polenta, pour the mixture onto a well-oiled baking tray to get a layer that is about 2cm thick. Refrigerate until cold. Then turn out and cut into desired shapes; at POLPO we usually make rectangles about 15cm × 5cm, or you can cut the polenta into triangles, which is quite authentic too.

Preheat the oven to 180°C/Gas 4. Oil the polenta shapes and place rough-side down on a medium-hot griddle pan. You could lightly pan-fry them if you don't have a griddle. When your little polenta slabs are nicely charred on both sides, remove them and place onto a baking tray and put into the preheated oven for 4–5 minutes to heat through.

PEAR, GORGONZOLA & CHICORY SALAD

The combination of ripe pears and blue cheese is a well-known treat and this salad is a lovely, fresh expression of those two strong flavours. There is an Italian proverb that sums up the specialness of this marriage: 'Al contadino non far sapere quanto è buono il formaggio con le pere.' (Don't tell the peasants how good cheese tastes with pears.)

You should avoid using young, creamy Gorgonzola as the vinegar in the dressing tends to melt it. Choose the more mature, crumbly variety which also has more piquancy.

For four to six:
100ml extra virgin olive oil
25ml red wine vinegar
1 tablespoon Dijon mustard
Flaky sea salt and black pepper
1 teaspoon caster sugar
150g mature Gorgonzola, cut into very small chunks
3 ripe pears – Comice is a good variety
1 large handful of curly endive
1 head of red chicory
1 head of white chicory

First make the mustard dressing. Put the olive oil, red wine vinegar, Dijon mustard, a small pinch of salt, a couple of grinds of pepper and the sugar into a bowl and whisk together. Add the very small chunks of Gorgonzola and mix them into the dressing.

Remove the core from the pears and then slice into thin discs (if you don't have a corer, just cut the pears in half, scoop out the core and cut the fruit into thin semi-circles). Place them in a large mixing bowl with washed curly endive, red and white chicory leaves and dress just enough to coat everything lightly. Turn over once or twice and then place gently onto your plates.

BEETROOT SALAD WITH ROCKET & WALNUT PESTO

Some people dismiss beetroot as boring, or even unpleasant, but I love it. Perhaps for them, there lingers too strong a memory of overly vinegary beetroots from a jar on the summer picnic blanket. To be honest, I even like those (try cutting them in quarters and mixing with off-the-shelf creamed horseradish for a tasty snack).

This salad is a colourful and tasty way to present beets and is a great excuse to make too much pesto. It keeps very well under a little oil and you can use it as you would any shop-bought pesto.

For six to eight:
2kg raw beetroot
50ml red wine vinegar
300g rocket leaves, washed and well dried
300g walnuts, roughly chopped
150g grated Parmesan
1½ tablespoons finely chopped garlic
Flaky sea salt and black pepper
Extra virgin olive oil

Boil the raw beetroots in plenty of water and a good splash of red wine vinegar. When tender (easily pierced with a knife) remove, allow to cool slightly and peel. Cut the beets into large bite-sized pieces.

In a large bowl mix the rocket, the chopped walnuts, grated Parmesan, chopped garlic and a good pinch of salt and grind of pepper.

Place half the mixture in a food processor. Pulse, slowly adding olive oil until the right consistency is achieved. You want the pesto to move slowly but not to pour like a liquid. Repeat with the other half. Combine the two batches and taste. Adjust the seasoning if necessary.

Dress the pieces of beetroot with a little pesto until they are lightly coated and serve.

FENNEL, FRENCH BEAN, CURLY ENDIVE & COBNUT SALAD

Cobnuts are part of the hazelnut family but are larger, wetter, paler and sweeter. They have a relatively short season, from August to November, and grow in abundance in Kent. In the US, filbert nuts, which are very similar, are grown commercially in Oregon. If you can't get hold of them, use fresh hazelnuts. Any of these nuts will work well in this salad.

The star of the show here is undoubtedly the very thinly sliced raw fennel and the amazing aniseed flavour it imparts. The curly endive and beans add great support and background to the strong flavours and texture. Instructions for blanching are on page 191, but be careful that you cook the beans almost through. French beans don't benefit from being under-cooked – they aren't pleasant to eat when they are too squeaky.

For four to six:
2 fennel bulbs
250g French beans
1 small curly endive, picked and washed
Flaky sea salt and black pepper
4 tablespoons extra virgin olive oil
2 tablespoon lemon juice
1 large handful of shelled cobnuts (or fresh hazelnuts)

Slice the fennel as finely as possible, using a mandoline if you can. Blanch the French beans for about 6–8 minutes, drain and plunge into cold water.

Mix the fennel, beans and curly endive with a pinch of salt, a grind of pepper, the olive oil and lemon juice. Add the nuts and serve.

GRILLED ZUCCHINI SALAD

This is a lovely way to prepare zucchini and helps to get rid of any leftover bread you have lurking in your bread bin. There is a satisfying chilli and garlic kick from the crumbs and I like the little crunch they add to the overall texture of the dish. If you have a griddle pan, you should use this — it makes smoky char-lines on the surface of the zucchini ribbons.

For four to six:
200g old bread
Extra virgin olive oil
1 garlic clove, finely chopped
1 teaspoon chilli flakes
Flaky sea salt and black pepper
6 zucchini
150g rocket leaves
Lemon juice

First, make the breadcrumbs. Preheat the oven to 180°C/Gas 4. Take the leftover bread and tear it into pieces. Place the bits of bread on a baking tray and pour on a good amount of olive oil. Shake the tray a few times and place in the oven. When the bread is crisp and golden, remove and let it cool. Place the toasted bread in a food processor with the chopped garlic, chilli flakes, and a pinch of salt and a grind of pepper. Whizz for a few seconds until the bread has turned into crumbs and tip into a bowl. Drop in a little more olive oil and turn a few times. You should taste and add more salt if necessary.

Slice the zucchini into long ribbons about 4mm thick. Season with salt, pepper and olive oil and then place onto a hot griddle pan (or use a normal pan). When the zucchini are charred and cooked through, remove them from the pan and let them come down to room temperature.

Dress the rocket leaves lightly with salt, lemon juice and olive oil and lay over the zucchini then scatter over the breadcrumbs.

ZUCCHINI SHOESTRING FRIES

For this recipe it is easy to convince yourself you are being virtuous. The zucchino is, after all, a vegetable.* It counts as one of your five-a-day, right? Well, I'm not so sure that the batter and deep-frying would convince a nutritionist but, good golly, these are tasty. Several of our customers come back to the restaurant specifically for this dish, happily admitting that they are addicted. Your habit starts here.

For four to six:
6 large zucchini
1 litre vegetable oil, for deep-frying
500ml cold milk
500g plain white flour, seasoned
A large pinch of fine salt

Using a comb attachment on a mandoline (if you have one), slice the zucchini lengthways to create fries 4mm across. Alternatively cut the zucchini by hand. The end raw result should be lengths of zucchini that look like shoestrings.

Half fill a deep pan with the oil and bring it up to 190°C (or until a cube of bread dropped in the oil turns golden in less than a minute). Carefully dredge the strings in the milk and shake around in the seasoned flour. Then place the fries in the boiling hot vegetable oil for 3 minutes, or until light brown. Drain the excess oil on kitchen paper and sprinkle with fine salt.

* Yes, I know it is actually a fruit, but let's not split hairs, eh?

FENNEL, RADISH & MINT WITH RICOTTA

This little salad is so light and delicate and pretty that it benefits from being served on tiny fancy plates or bowls. You can always have a second helping.

For four to six:
400g ricotta
Flaky sea salt and black pepper
100ml extra virgin olive oil, plus a little for the ricotta
2 fennel bulbs
12 red breakfast radishes
1 small handful of mint leaves, roughly chopped
Juice of 1 lemon

Season the ricotta with a little salt, pepper and olive oil. Smear a generous spoonful onto your plates to create a wide blob in the centre of each one.

Using a mandoline if you have one, slice the fennel and radishes as finely as possible and place them in a bowl. Add the chopped mint, a pinch of salt, a grind of pepper, the olive oil and the lemon juice and turn very gently in the bowl until everything is lightly coated. Place on top of the ricotta. It really is that simple.

MOZZARELLA PIZZAIOLA

Pizzaiola is a Neapolitan sauce and is usually used in Carne Pizzaiola, a humble dish consisting of meat, tomatoes and oregano. We make a similar tomato and oregano sauce but serve it with a whole mozzarella ball. You can serve this on a simple salad of rocket leaves, if you like.

For four:
2kg tomatoes — any firm variety
Extra virgin olive oil
Red wine vinegar
Flaky sea salt and black pepper
2 tablespoons caster sugar
1 handful of oregano leaves
4 × 125g balls of buffalo mozzarella

Preheat the oven to 140°C/Gas 1. Cut the tomatoes into bite-sized pieces and lay in a single layer on a baking tray. Pour over several good glugs of olive oil, a couple of good splashes of red wine vinegar, a pinch of salt, a grind of pepper, the sugar and half the oregano. Roast in the low oven for 1½ hrs or until the tomatoes are only just holding their shape. Check the seasoning. The tomatoes should be wonderfully sweet and sharp.

Place equal amounts of the tomato onto four plates and scatter with the remaining oregano, chopped this time. Place a whole buffalo mozzarella ball in the centre and dress with a short drizzle of olive oil.

BURRATA WITH LENTILS & BASIL OIL

Burrata is often confused with mozzarella but they are not the same. Burrata is made in Puglia with milk from Razza Podolica cows (not buffalo) and with added cream, so it is softer and more moist than mozzarella. Burrata's creamy, sweet consistency is the perfect foil to an array of ingredients. It is a delight with bitter cime di rapa, for example. This recipe combines it with lentils — a heavenly marriage. Make sure your burrata is of the finest quality and at room temperature. Serving it fridge-cold kills the texture and the flavour.

For six:
Leaves from a bunch of basil
Flaky sea salt and black pepper
Extra virgin olive oil
400g Puy lentils
2 large carrots, finely chopped
3 celery sticks, finely chopped
1 small onion, finely chopped
3 garlic cloves, finely chopped
5 sprigs of thyme, leaves removed and chopped
4 tablespoons mustard dressing – in the recipe for Pear,
    Gorgonzola & Chicory Salad, see page 207
6 burrata balls

First make the basil oil by placing most of the basil leaves in a food processor, reserving a few of the smaller prettier ones for decorating at the end. Add a little salt and enough olive oil to make a thin sauce. Whizz for a few seconds and then set aside.

Put the lentils in a saucepan with enough cold water to cover them by about 7cm. Don't add salt at this stage as this will toughen the lentils. Bring to the boil and cook for about 45 minutes. Keep checking them – they need to still hold a small bite. When they are done, drain, refresh in cold water, drain again and set aside.

Now, in a large heavy-based pan sweat the vegetables in a few good glugs of olive oil with the thyme leaves, a large pinch of salt and a twist of ground black pepper. When the vegetables are softened and translucent, add the cooked lentils and a splash of water to stop them sticking to the bottom of the pan.

Make the mustard dressing in the Pear, Chicory and Gorgonzola Salad (you'll need a third of this quantity).

To finish the dish, add 4 tablespoons of the mustard dressing to the lentils, check the seasoning and spoon onto a large warm plate. Then tear open your burrata and place on top of the warm lentils. The heat from the lentils will melt the burrata making it even more creamy and soft.

Drizzle some basil oil over the top and scatter with the reserved basil leaves.

WHITE BEANS
& WILD GARLIC

Wild garlic is one of those plants that you will often come across on a woodland walk. The flowers are very pretty, with small white petals, and the aroma is unmistakably of garlic. I can never resist foraging then-and-there when I find them. The flavour is subtle, less pungent than garlic cloves alone, and is delicious here with velvety cannellini beans.

For four to six:
200g dried cannellini beans
1 onion, cut in half
2 bay leaves
1 head of garlic, cut in half
Flaky sea salt and black pepper
Extra virgin olive oil
1 bunch of wild garlic leaves, de-stalked and roughly chopped

Soak the cannellini beans overnight in plenty of water. The next day drain and wash the beans and place in a large pan with enough water to cover by a good 3cm. Do not add salt. Place the onion halves, bay leaves and the halved head of garlic in the pan. Bring to a rapid boil and skim off any floating scum. Reduce the heat and let everything simmer till the beans are cooked through – this could be up to 1½ hours.

When the beans are cooked, remove and discard the onion, garlic and bay leaves, and drain, retaining a little of the remaining cooking liquid. Make sure you season the beans with salt and pepper while they are still warm.

Reheat the beans in a little of their cooking liquid and a good splash of olive oil, throw in the roughly chopped wild garlic leaves and adjust the seasoning. After 2 minutes, remove from the heat and serve.

SPINACH, CHILLI & GARLIC

This little dish is the perfect accompaniment to fish or meat. It goes particularly well with subtle, white, fleshy fish such as bream or with a simple grilled chop. I love it with veal. The quantity of chilli you use is entirely personal.

For each person:
250g washed young spinach, large stalks removed
Extra virgin olive oil
Pinch of finely chopped garlic
Pinch of dried chilli flakes, to taste
Flaky sea salt and black pepper

Simply blanch your spinach for about 2 minutes and refresh in cold water. Drain and roughly chop.

Heat a good glug of olive oil in a large frying pan with the finely chopped garlic and dried chilli flakes. When the oil is hot, but before the garlic browns, throw in the spinach, some salt and pepper and a little water to stop the spinach from sticking to the pan. Turn a few times, remove from the heat and serve (you will have to squeeze out excess liquid before the plate goes on the table).

ITALIAN CHICORY WITH ANCHOVY DRESSING

Italian chicory (cicoria in Italian) is very different from the closed endive we are used to seeing in supermarkets. It is more flower-like and has long variegated green fronds that resemble larger, plumper dandelion leaves. It makes me envious when I walk round the markets of Venice, Treviso, Padua and Verona – on flying back to London my hand luggage is often a brimming bag of greengroceries.

If you can't find cicoria, this anchovy dressing works well on most lightly cooked green vegetables or raw endive.

For four to six:
2 medium free-range egg yolks
1 tablespoon Dijon mustard
12 brown anchovy fillets
5 basil leaves
Small pinch of chilli flakes
2 tablespoons red wine vinegar
250ml vegetable oil
2 heads of Italian chicory (cicoria)
About 50ml garlic-infused oil – in the recipe for
    Baccalà Mantecato, see page 38
Flaky sea salt and black pepper

To make the anchovy dressing, place the egg yolks, Dijon mustard, anchovies, basil leaves, chilli flakes and red wine vinegar into a food processor. Blend briefly until all the ingredients are well combined. With the motor running, slowly add the vegetable oil and then trickle in a little water until you have a pouring consistency that is about the same as double cream.

Preheat the oven to 190°C/Gas 5. Cut the chicory into 8cm pieces on the diagonal. Blanch the harder white bits for 3 minutes until soft but still retaining a little bite then refresh in cold water. Blanch the softer green leafier parts for 2 minutes and refresh in cold water. Dress the leaves with a little garlic-infused olive oil, salt and pepper.

To serve, place the chicory on a baking tray and heat for a few minutes in the hot oven, to warm through. Remove and place on a serving plate. Drizzle with the anchovy dressing.

You can also serve this dish with added melted mozzarella. Simply place some pieces of good quality mozzarella on top of the chicory before you put it into the oven to heat.

ASPARAGUS WITH PARMESAN & ANCHOVY BUTTER

Chefs get very excited by asparagus. More than any other vegetable, it heralds the arrival of spring. It is usually around the second or third week of April that someone or other will announce the arrival of new season asparagus.

Aside from the symbolic seasonal significance of asparagus, it is delicious, versatile and as pretty a vegetable as you are going to find. It is particularly at home in risotto — see page 234.

For eight:
125g unsalted butter — at room temperature
12 brown anchovy fillets, roughly chopped
½ garlic clove, finely chopped
Small pinch of chilli flakes
6 basil leaves, roughly chopped
40 asparagus spears
1 large handful of shaved Parmesan

Let's start with the anchovy butter. Put the butter in a food processor and blend with the anchovy fillets, chopped garlic, chilli flakes and chopped basil leaves. Remove this very soft butter mixture and chill.

Preheat the oven to 160°C/Gas 3. Trim the asparagus spears at their tough, woody ends, using a potato peeler so they taper. Blanch for approximately 3 minutes until tender and then refresh in cold water. Set aside.

Place the spears on a baking tray and heat in the oven for 5 minutes. Transfer the asparagus to a handsome serving dish and place several knobs of the anchovy butter on top. Scatter over the Parmesan and serve immediately.

BORLOTTI BEANS, SAVOY CABBAGE & ROSEMARY BREADCRUMBS

This combination works rather well because the hearty cabbage brings texture, the beans bring a lovely buttery flavour and the rosemary adds a slightly spicy, aromatic quality. Oh, and I like the crunch from the breadcrumbs too.

For four to six:
200g dried borlotti beans
1 onion, cut in half
4 sprigs of rosemary, 2 left whole and leaves from
    2 chopped
2 bay leaves
2 garlic cloves, 1 cut in half and 1 chopped
100g old bread
Extra virgin olive oil
Flaky sea salt and black pepper
Zest of 1 lemon
1 small Savoy cabbage, cored and leaves separated

Soak the borlotti beans overnight in plenty of water. The next day drain and wash the beans and place in a large pan with enough water to cover by a good 3 cm. Place the onion halves in the water along with the whole rosemary sprigs, the bay leaves and the halved garlic clove. Bring to a rapid boil and skim off any floating scum. Reduce the heat and simmer till the beans are cooked through – about 1½ hours. Remember to add more water if the level drops.

Whilst the beans are cooking, make the breadcrumbs. Preheat the oven to 180°C/Gas 4. Take the bread and tear it into pieces. Place the bits of bread on a baking tray and pour on a good amount of olive oil and sprinkle on the chopped rosemary. Shake the tray a few times and place in the oven. When the bread is crisp and golden, remove and let it cool. Place the toasted bread in a food processor with the chopped garlic and a pinch of salt and pepper. Whizz for a few seconds until the bread has turned into crumbs and turn out into a bowl. Drop in a little more olive oil and turn a few times. Add the lemon zest, mix, taste and adjust the seasoning.

When the beans have cooked, remove and discard the herbs, onion and garlic. Drain, retaining a little of the cooking liquid. Season with salt and pepper.

Cut the Savoy cabbage leaves into thick strips and blanch in boiling water for a few minutes until tender. Drop into ice-cold water. Drain and set aside.

To serve, reheat the beans in a little of their cooking liquid and a good splash of olive oil, throw in the blanched cabbage and simmer for just a few moments. Scatter generously with the rosemary breadcrumbs.

RÌSI E BÌSI

This is a dish that means a lot to Venetians. It is the principal offering at the annual feast to celebrate the city's patron saint, Saint Mark the Evangelist. The feast day is 25 April and tradition has it that the very first young peas of the season are used for this delightful and simple risotto. To make an authentic Rìsi e Bìsi you need to use young peas, the smallest and tenderest you can find. This is not one of those dishes where frozen peas will do. Absolutely not. Sorry. You must use fresh peas. And you must shell them. You may want to buy twenty per cent more peas than you actually need so that you can reward yourself whilst shelling by popping the occasional raw pea in your mouth.

For six:
2kg fresh peas in their pods
2 onions, 1 cut in half and 1 finely chopped
Flaky sea salt and black pepper
50ml extra virgin olive oil
60g unsalted butter
150g small pancetta lardons (optional)
400g risotto rice – carnaroli is best
1 handful of mint leaves, chopped
1 handful of flat parsley leaves, chopped
1 large handful of grated Parmesan

Shell the peas in advance because you are going to make a simple stock with the empty pods. In a large pan, bring 2.5 litres of water to the boil. When all the peas are shelled, place the pods (but not the peas) in the pan with the halved onion. (Move the freshly podded peas to one side, out of temptation's way.) Bring the pods to the boil for only a minute or two and then take off the heat. Remove and discard the pods. Now you have your stock for making the risotto.

Sweat the finely chopped onion with a few pinches of salt in the olive oil and half the butter in a heavy-based pan. This should be a slow process on a low heat – you don't want it to turn brown at all. The onion should become clear, shiny and translucent. Add the pancetta lardons, if using, and continue to sauté for a few minutes. Add a twist of black pepper.

Now add the rice and stir slowly for 2 minutes. You want to coat every grain in the oil and butter so that everything looks glossy and nothing is sticking. With a large ladle, put just enough stock in the pan to cover everything but not drown it. The contents will let off a satisfying hiss and a cloud of steam. This first ladleful will be absorbed and evaporate very quickly. Add another. If the pan continues to bubble, the heat is too high. Turn it down and stir slowly.

For the next 15 minutes or so you should continue to stir slowly and add a ladleful of stock every time the rice looks less than wet. You are continually letting the rice absorb the liquid and allowing the grains to release their starch. Towards the end, add the peas, half the chopped mint and half the chopped parsley. Taste and add more salt if needed, but not too much. Remember that the Parmesan will add a little salt to the balance.

Don't be a slave to the clock; taste your grains to know when they are done. They should still have a little bite to them. When they are ready, make sure the mixture is nice and runny. Unlike a regular risotto, Rìsi e Bisi should be more liquid, rather like a thick soup. Take off the heat. Gently stir in the Parmesan, the remaining butter, mint and parsley. Cover the pan and let it rest for a few minutes, and then serve in wide shallow bowls.

CHICKPEA, LEEK & FENNEL SOUP

A hearty soup can be a meal in its own right. I will quite happily sit down to supper with a large bowl of steaming soup, a hunk of bread and want for nothing else. Chickpeas are known in parts of Italy as 'carne dei poveri' (paupers' meat) and although this dish is satisfyingly inexpensive to make, I find the combination of ingredients quite sophisticated; subtle but still incredibly flavoursome. I will often make this soup to cheer myself up on a rainy day.

For six to eight:
500g dried chickpeas (or 2 × 400g tins)
2 litres chicken stock
A pinch of dried chilli
Extra virgin olive oil
2 shallots, finely diced
2 leeks, cut into 1cm pieces
2 small fennel bulbs, cut into 1cm pieces
Flaky sea salt and black pepper

Cover the chickpeas in water and soak overnight. In the morning, drain and transfer to a heavy-based pan with the chicken stock. There should be enough stock to cover the chickpeas by at least 3cm. Add a pinch of dried chilli, and cook until tender.

In a separate large heavy-based pan heat a little olive oil and in it sweat the shallots, leeks and fennel until soft. Season with salt and pepper. Combine the chickpeas, including the stock, and the vegetables and simmer for 5 minutes. (If you don't have enough time to soak and cook the chickpeas, you can use tinned chickpeas here instead, well drained and rinsed.)

Remove a quarter of the vegetables and chickpeas and set to one side. Blend the remainder of the chickpea and vegetable mixture until smooth. Add the whole chickpeas and vegetables back to the soup and season to taste. Serve with a dash of good olive oil.

BUTTERNUT RISOTTO

*We have experimented with various pumpkins and squashes in this risotto,
including exotic Italian varieties such as Chioggia and smaller, rarer types like
Green Acorn or Iron Bark – all very good. Forget those huge orange Halloween
pumpkins though. They should really only be used for making lanterns – the
flesh is stringy and the flavour unconvincing. But the most convenient and
common is butternut squash. It is easy to get hold of and you achieve a consistent,
smooth and creamy result when cooking with it.*

For four to six:
1 medium (1kg) butternut squash
Flaky sea salt and black pepper
Extra virgin olive oil
8 sage leaves, torn
2 large onions, 1 roughly chopped and 1 finely chopped
3 celery sticks, roughly chopped
2 carrots, roughly chopped
10 peppercorns
2 bay leaves
50g unsalted butter – at room temperature
300g risotto rice – carnaroli is best
A glass of dry vermouth
50g grated Parmesan

Preheat the oven to 200°C/Gas 6. Peel the butternut squash and cut into
2cm squares, discarding all the seeds and fibre but not the skin and stalk
– you want to keep these for your stock. Place the cut pieces of squash
on a baking tray and season with salt, pepper and several good glugs of
olive oil. Scatter over the torn sage leaves. Cover with foil and bake in
the preheated oven for 20–30 minutes, or until cooked through. Remove
when ready, cover and set aside.

For the stock, take the squash peelings and stalk, the roughly chopped
onion, celery, carrots, peppercorns and bay leaves and place in 2 litres
of cold water in a large, heavy-based pan. Slowly bring to the boil and
when it's boiling rapidly, turn the heat off. After 30 minutes, strain out
the vegetables, peppercorns and bay leaves and discard, leaving a lovely
golden stock. Pour back into the saucepan and have ready for the risotto.

Pour a glug of olive oil into a large, heavy-based pan with 20g of the
butter and slowly sauté the finely chopped onion until the onion becomes
translucent and glossy. This will take about 15 minutes on low heat.
Don't let the onions turn brown. Heat up the stock again. Add the rice
to the onions and stir for 2 minutes, coating every grain. Add the glass

of vermouth. It will create a cloud of steam and a hiss and evaporate quite quickly. But doesn't it smell amazing?

Add a large ladle of the hot stock and let the rice absorb the liquid, stirring all the while. Add another ladle to cover the rice and repeat this process as the rice absorbs the stock and the grains release their starch and the whole mixture takes on a delightful creamy consistency. After 15 minutes or so, taste the rice – it should be creamy but still have a slight bite.

When the rice is done, remove from the heat and carefully fold in the Parmesan, the remaining butter and the roasted squash. Cover and let the whole thing rest for a few minutes and then serve.

ASPARAGUS RISOTTO WITH PROSCIUTTO

The first time I met Enrica Rocca was at POLPO when she told me off for serving capers in an octopus salad. She is a respected authority on Venetian cooking and one of the champions of authenticity, simplicity and honesty in Italian cuisine.

She regularly holds cooking classes in the modern studio that backs onto her family's palazzo on Zattere in Dorsoduro. When I called her one time from Marco Polo airport, her directions were very specific: 'Go over the bridge at Calcina, turn left then take the first right, darling. Walk along the alley to the end, mine is the last door on the right. You can't miss it, darling. It's Ferrari red!'

As well as her famous cookery classes in Venice, Enrica holds demonstrations in London, too, where she has had a long connection with Borough Market. In fact, the way she works in both cities is remarkably similar. One February morning I met her by the Ponte de la Calcina and we walked to Rialto Market together. She is an efficient shopper, homing in on market traders, assessing their wares, rubbing her jaw as she deliberates and finally either making a purchase or moving on to the next stall.

This is a risotto Enrica made for me one late spring morning.

For four to six:
50g unsalted butter
Extra virgin olive oil
1 large white onion, finely chopped
A glass of white wine
2 litres chicken stock
A large bunch of asparagus
300g risotto rice – carnaroli is best
Black pepper
1 handful of grated Parmesan, plus extra to serve
4–6 very thin slices of prosciutto

Put 10g of the butter and 1 tablespoon of olive oil in a deep, heavy-based saucepan over a low heat and in it sweat the onion for 15–20 minutes, or until transparent. Add the glass of white wine and gently cook for a further 5 minutes. Meanwhile, bring the chicken stock up to a simmer in a separate pan.

Cut the woody stalks off the asparagus spears and discard. Blanch half the asparagus spears in salted boiling water for 3 minutes then refresh them in cold water and set aside. Chop the other half of the asparagus into pieces.

Now, back to your main pan: add the rice and asparagus pieces to the onions and coat each grain in the juices. Twist a little pepper into the rice and stir. Add a ladleful of stock to cover the rice and stir. Continue to add stock and stir slowly, never letting the rice absorb all the stock.

When the rice has reached the right 'bite', probably after 15 minutes or so, add the Parmesan and the remaining butter. Stir 4 or 5 times, slowly, so that butter melts and Parmesan is absorbed into rice. Take off the heat and cover the pan with a lid. Let it rest for a few minutes. Serve onto large plates, dress with the remaining blanched spears of asparagus, lay over a single slice of very thin prosciutto and scatter with some more grated Parmesan.

RUNNER BEANS WITH RED ONION & PECORINO

Here is a delightful summery salad that is easy to prepare and looks as vibrant as it tastes. The runner beans take on a particularly intense green hue after blanching and look great on a picnic table next to tomatoes, for example. Be careful not to overdo (or underdo) the beans — they should still have some bite but not be too squeaky.

For four to six:
500g runner beans
1 small red onion
Flaky sea salt and black pepper
Extra virgin olive oil
200g Pecorino Romano

Run a peeler down the sides of the runner beans to remove their string. Chop at an angle into 3cm pieces. Blanch in salted boiling water for 3 minutes or until tender and then refresh in cold water.

Finely slice the red onion and place in a large mixing bowl with a pinch of salt to draw out some bitterness. Now add the blanched runner beans with a twist of black pepper and a glug of good olive oil. Turn a few times to coat and taste. Add salt if needed but remember that the cheese is quite salty anyway.

Gently place the dressed runner beans and onion into your prettiest serving dish and shave the Pecorino Romano over the top.

PIEDMONTESE PEPPERS & WHITE ANCHOVIES

This is a great way to present peppers. You normally see them raw as a salad ingredient and, I have to confess, they leave me a bit cold; I find them bland and watery. But when roasted, they yield a sweet juice and the flesh becomes silky and interesting. It is important to leave the stalks intact in this recipe, not because they are edible (they are not) but because it helps the pepper halves retain their shape. The juices are substantial and delicious – make sure you spoon them from the roasting tray onto the serving dishes. And don't forget to mop up with good bread.

For four:
2 medium tomatoes
2 large red peppers
Flaky sea salt and black pepper
1 garlic clove, thinly sliced
Extra virgin olive oil
1 small handful of basil leaves
12–16 white anchovy fillets – at room temperature

Preheat the oven to 160°C/Gas 3. Put the kettle on. Make a small cross in the bottom of each tomato and place them in a bowl. Submerge the tomatoes in boiling water and leave to sit for 30 seconds. Carefully remove them from the water and place under cool running water. Peel the tomatoes and cut into quarters.

Take the red peppers and cut them in half lengthways, through the stem. Scoop out the seeds and core and discard. Place them on a baking tray, cut-side up. Place 2 quarters of tomato into each pepper half, season with a little salt and black pepper and add to each one a few slivers of thinly sliced garlic and a good drizzle of olive oil. Bake in the preheated oven for about 40 minutes, or until cooked through but just holding their shape.

Remove the peppers from the oven and dress with a few torn basil leaves and three or four white anchovy fillets in each one. Drizzle on a little olive oil and serve.

TREVISO RISOTTO

The first time I made this dish was after a miserable trip to Venice one January. It rained the whole time, I was on my own and feeling sorry for myself. The one redeeming aspect of the trip was that I bought a couple of kilos of Treviso Tardivo (the variety of radicchio with tentacle-like purple and white leaves) from a market stall and stuffed the veg into my cabin baggage. Back home I found a quirky recipe for radicchio risotto that used pancetta and beef stock. I made an improvised version and was eating it a mere five hours after leaving Italy. It was delicious.

On a trip to Friuli shortly afterwards, I was fortunate enough to dine at the home of a winemaker who was also an enthusiastic cook. He made a risotto of such remarkable creaminess that I asked what it was that he had done differently. 'I make all my dishes in the traditional way,' he announced. What was that? I asked. 'I never use olive oil!'

Quite an arresting statement coming from an Italian, I thought, but the winemaker went on to explain that less than a century ago, the south and the north of Italy were virtually two separate nations. Among many other differences, the south produced the fat it needed for cooking by pressing olives for oil and the north produced its cooking fat by churning milk into butter.

Only in the early decades of the twentieth century was the distribution of the near miraculous olive oil substantial enough for the whole nation to use it. Up to then, the northern Italians, without refrigeration, would clarify their butter, scrape the impurities and scum from the surface, and use that to cook with.

Every other recipe for risotto I have seen uses butter and olive oil together. This one requires only butter.

For four to six:
2 litres good stock – chicken or vegetable
100g unsalted butter – at room temperature
1 sprig of rosemary
1 onion, finely chopped
300g risotto rice – carnaroli is best
Flaky sea salt
A glass of dry vermouth
500g Treviso Tardivo radicchio, cut into 3cm pieces
75g grated Parmesan

Get your stock simmering gently in a pan. Put two-thirds of the butter and the rosemary sprig into a heavy-based pan on a low to medium heat. When the butter has melted and starts to get hot, swirl the rosemary around several times to flavour the butter and then remove and discard. Add the chopped onion and sauté slowly until glossy and translucent (about 10–15 minutes).

Now add the rice and make sure every grain is coated in butter. Mix gently in with the onions, taking care that nothing burns or sticks. Add a pinch of salt.

You can now throw in your glass of vermouth with a flourish; you will be rewarded with a loud hiss and a cloud of steam. Keep stirring, making sure nothing sticks. The vermouth doesn't last long – it is absorbed and evaporated in a matter of minutes.

Add your first ladleful of stock to cover the rice and stir. If the mixture is bubbling, turn the heat down. It should just be simmering gently.

Remove a small handful of the finest and most delicate pieces of the radicchio and set aside. Place the remaining majority into the mixture, stir and add another ladle of stock.

Stay with your risotto for another 15 minutes, adding a little stock at a time, only when the rice has absorbed the last ladleful. Taste, adjust seasoning if necessary, and make sure the grains have a tiny amount of bite still in them. The risotto should not be too thick. You want it to ooze. When ready, remove from the heat, fold in the remaining butter, the Parmesan and the small leaves you earlier set aside, cover and leave for a few minutes before serving.

PASTA, BEANS & ROSEMARY OIL

This is peasant food of the most warming and comforting kind. It is really a soup, but a particularly thick one. You will find as many different versions of this dish as there are types of pasta. In fact, I have seen this made with tagliatelle, bigoli and penne, none of which seem right to me. I like the pasta to be roughly the same size as the beans. At POLPO we use macaroni and we finish with a little rosemary oil as an aromatic flourish.

For six to eight:
500g dried borlotti beans
1 handful of rosemary
1 garlic clove, halved
1 onion, cut into wedges
Flaky sea salt and black pepper
200ml extra virgin olive oil, plus extra for beans
1 litre tomato sauce – see page 149
150g small dried macaroni

Soak the dried beans overnight in cold water. Rinse and drain the beans and place them in a large, heavy-based saucepan. Add water to cover the beans by about 3cm and put in half the rosemary sprigs, 1 garlic half and the onion. Bring to the boil, reduce the heat to a simmer and cover with a lid. Cook until tender (probably about 45 minutes–1 hour) then drain, remove the garlic and onion and season while still warm. Add a nice splash of olive oil. Set aside.

To make the rosemary oil, chop the leaves from the rest of the rosemary as finely as possible, place them in a deep bowl with a pinch of salt and the remaining garlic half, finely chopped, and the olive oil. Combine and taste. Set aside.

Gently heat the tomato sauce in a separate pan while cooking the macaroni in plenty of salted water until they are just al dente. Drain the pasta, throw it into the heavy-bottomed pan with the beans and then add enough of the tomato sauce to the beans and cooked pasta to create a thick soup. Check the seasoning and ladle into large soup bowls.

Spoon a little of the rosemary oil over each bowl of the thick soup before serving.

CAULIFLOWER & FONTINA GRATIN

This is a particularly good accompaniment to a rich meat such as braised ox cheeks (see page 172), or can be served as a dish in its own right. It is an indulgent and comforting use of a much underused and unloved vegetable, the humble cauliflower.

We sometimes like to make this dish with a topping of herby breadcrumbs, added in the final 10 to 15 minutes of cooking. Use the breadcrumb recipe on page 212, with the addition of a small handful of finely chopped flat parsley.

For four to six:
1 large cauliflower
400ml milk
1 onion, sliced
10 whole black peppercorns
1 bay leaf
40g unsalted butter
20g plain white flour
Flaky sea salt and black pepper
150g Fontina, derinded and grated
100g Parmesan, grated
100g block mozzarella, grated

Take the cauliflower and trim off the larger leaves. Cut the body into florets of equal sizes. Blanch the florets until they are just tender, but no more – about 4 minutes or so – and then refresh in cold water. (The cooking time will depend on the size of the florets, but please check one and make sure you do not overcook them.) Drain the cauliflower and place in a large earthenware dish or roasting tray with the florets facing up.

To make the cheese sauce, heat the milk in a small pan with the sliced onion, peppercorns and bay leaf. Simmer for a few minutes and then strain and set aside.

Preheat the oven to 200°C/Gas 6. Melt the butter slowly in a separate pan, taking care is does not burn. Add the flour slowly, stirring all the time with a wooden spoon to make a smooth paste. Pour the infused milk little by little and whisk with your spoon. Continue adding the milk slowly until about half is in.

Now you must upgrade your weapon and take a proper whisk and start whisking briskly while adding the rest of the milk until you get a lovely creamy sauce. Add a pinch of salt and a twist of black pepper. Take the heat right down, simmer for 5 minutes or so while whisking and check the seasoning. Now add the cheese, retaining 50g of the Fontina, and stir until the cheese is melted. Let the sauce simmer for another 5 minutes and then remove from the heat.

Pour the cheese sauce over the cauliflower and scatter the remaining Fontina over the top. Place in the preheated oven for about 10–15 minutes until the dish is golden brown and bubbling hot, but let it cool slightly before you eat it; I have burnt the roof of my mouth with impatience too many times to count. Add a final twist of black pepper before you serve.

CAPONATA

*This Sicilian staple is a fantastic accompaniment to any meal, its deep,
rich flavours a reminder of the sun-soaked island of its origin. I have never
seen it served in Venice but we made this version at POLPO in our first
summer and it was a huge hit. Traditionally it contains olives, but I prefer
this simpler version.*

*Caponata can be eaten on its own or as an accompaniment to a wide
range of meats and fish.*

For eight to ten:
3 medium aubergines
Extra virgin olive oil
6 celery sticks, peeled of their string and cut on the diagonal
      into 2cm pieces
2 red onions, cut into thin wedges
1 handful of capers
1.5kg tomatoes, quartered
3 garlic cloves, chopped
100ml red wine vinegar
30g caster sugar
Flaky sea salt and black pepper
1 handful of basil leaves, roughly torn

De-stalk and cut the aubergines into largish chunks of about 3cm.
Heat a large heavy pan with 1cm of olive oil and fry the pieces in two
batches until golden brown. Remove from the oil and set aside.

Preheat the oven to 160°C/Gas 3. Using the same pan, sweat the celery,
onion and capers in the olive oil, with a good pinch of salt and pepper.
When everything is soft and shiny (about 10 minutes), remove from the
pan and place in a large roasting tray with the cooked aubergine. Scatter
over the tomatoes and chopped garlic and pour over the red wine vinegar.
Add the sugar, salt and pepper.

Put in the preheated oven for about 1 hour or until the tomatoes
have lost some of their moisture and are almost disintegrating.
Stir everything together.

Serve warm or at room temperature (never hot) with the torn basil
leaves folded through it.

DESSERTS

Italians don't do fancy puddings. You will rarely see elaborate creations of the kind served in, say, French restaurants. Instead, there might be a cake, like the classic polenta cake Pinza, or any one of a vast array of biscuity things, such as Ciambella. There will certainly be good ice cream.

Venice has an interesting relationship with its desserts. Nearly all of them are connected to a time of the year or to a festival. Indeed, several have a religious significance that many people in the city and the region still recognize. Carnevale and Easter in particular are occasions when Venice's kitchens fill with the warm smell of baked treats: Fugassa Pasquale, the sweet and slightly spicy bread that is shaped like a dove; Essi, cute cookies in the form of the letter 'S'; Galani and Fritole, sinful little doughnuts that you find in abundance around Shrove Tuesday.

There are other fascinating Venetian specialities that have not made it onto the menu at POLPO and do not appear in this book but for which you should keep a lookout in the confectionery shops and bakeries of Venice when you visit. Venetian fried custard is something of a local treasure and fairly easy to find. Fave alla Veneziana are little coloured sugar bombs in the shape of beans that are made in November around All Saints' Day.

Incidentally, you will find lots of marzipan in Venice and I only recently discovered why: it originates from the city. Its Venetian name is marzapane – in other words, Pane di San Marco, or St Mark's Bread.

I like desserts that don't require lots of time to make, and I especially like those that can be prepared simply in advance. This is the ideal way to plan a dinner party, too. You don't want any stress at the end of the meal worrying that your soufflé might not rise.

Many Italian desserts involve booze: biscuits dipped in Vin Santo, Prosecco mixed with sorbet, grappa mixed with coffee, sponge soaked in rum. And those that don't include alcohol are very often accompanied by it; it is almost unthinkable to finish a meal in Italy without a small glass of grappa. You may want to keep a bottle in the house, you know, just in case.

AFFOGATO AL CAFFÈ

I have put this brilliant concoction first for good reason; it is a sensation. Really.
Don't bother with the rest of this section, in fact. This simple dessert, if you
can call it that, works every time for me.

Simply place a scoop of vanilla ice cream into a small glass or cup and, at
the table, pour over a really strong, really good single espresso. That's it.

SGROPPINO

This is another really neat combination. It is, effectively, a sophisticated Slush Puppy.

For each person put one large scoop of lemon sorbet into a blender with 100ml Prosecco. Whizz briefly and pour into a chilled glass. You can do the same thing in a bowl with a hand whisk if you prefer.

For a Sgroppino Corretto ('corrected' Sgroppino) simply add a 25ml shot of vodka per person to the mix. Or you can try adding a measure of Campari, or a fruit purée, such as strawberry or peach, to make a Bellini Sgroppino.

FLOURLESS ORANGE & ALMOND CAKE

This is a perfect sweet accompaniment to coffee. The firm and tangy orange sponge and zesty sauce really perk up the taste buds at the end of the meal. In addition, this dessert substitutes flour with ground almonds so it is suitable for those who can't or don't eat wheat. It's ideal for preparing in advance. All you have to do is slice and finish with the syrup and mascarpone cream.

For twelve slices:
2 oranges
100g brown sugar
400g caster sugar
6 medium free-range eggs
250g ground almonds
1½ teaspoons baking powder
Zest and juice of 1 orange
250g mascarpone
2 tablespoons double cream

Place the 2 oranges into a large pan with plenty of water and boil gently for 2 hours. Remove the oranges and set aside. Reserve the cooking liquid.

Place the brown sugar and half the caster sugar into a food processor and crack in the eggs. Whizz until white and fluffy.

Preheat the oven to 180°C/Gas 4. When the oranges have cooled enough to handle, roughly cut them into medium-sized pieces, remove any seeds and add to the processor. Now continue to whizz until smooth. Add the ground almonds and baking powder and whizz to combine.

Grease a 26cm cake tin with oil and line with baking parchment. Pour the smooth mixture from the processor into the tin and bake in the preheated oven for 1–1½ hours. Test the cake by skewering the centre with a clean metal skewer. If it comes back out clean and dry then the cake is cooked.

To make the syrup, pour the reserved cooking liquid from the oranges into a large pan. Use water to top up to 750ml if there is not enough liquid. Add the remaining caster sugar, the zest of an orange, cut into very thin strips and then its juice. Bring to a fierce boil for 10 minutes or until thick and syrupy, not forgetting it will thicken more once taken off the heat.

Mix the mascarpone with the double cream. To serve, slice the cake and place a little of the mascarpone cream on the side. Dress with the syrup.

TIRAMISÙ POTS

Tiramisù is probably the best known of all Italian desserts and its origins are local – by most accounts it was first created in Treviso at a restaurant called Le Beccherie. It is a reasonably recent invention, too, probably dating only from the 1970s. And yet already it has had the chance to be completely debased. Tiramisù can go badly wrong when messed about with. I recently had a shocking 'deconstructed' version at a very famous restaurant, but it is a delightful combination when done properly. The name translates as 'pick-me-up' and, rather than feeling heavy and rich, it should tantalize and leave you wanting more.

Often tiramisù is made in a large tray and then portioned into squares, like lasagne. We prefer to make them individually in 150ml Duralex tumblers. They refrigerate better and are somehow more fun to eat. I recommend you buy a dozen or more tumblers like this as they have so many uses (not least for wine).

For twelve pots:
6 double espressos (or 360ml very strong coffee), warm
4 tablespoons dark rum
250g caster sugar
6 medium free-range eggs, separated
120ml Marsala
500g mascarpone
1 packet of Savoiardi sponge fingers (you need 24 biscuits)
Cocoa powder

Start by combining the warm espresso coffee with the rum and 50g of the sugar. Stir until the sugar has dissolved. Set aside.

Separate the eggs and reserve the yolks in a large bowl. In another clean bowl, whisk the whites until they are stiff. Add the remaining sugar and the Marsala to the yolks. Whisk until pale and fluffy, add the mascarpone and gently stir it in. Fold the whisked whites into the yolk mixture.

For each glass you will need approximately 2 sponge fingers. Dip a sponge finger in the coffee mixture and let it absorb enough of the liquid to wet the whole thing without breaking it up. Place one half in the bottom of your glass. Spoon over 1 tablespoon of the mascarpone cream. Place the other half biscuit on top and spoon over another tablespoon of cream. At this point sprinkle over a little cocoa powder. Take another sodden sponge finger, break in two and lay both halves on top. Cover in a little more cream. Repeat this for all 12 glasses and store, covered in the fridge, for no fewer than 8 hours, so they are properly set.

Just before serving, liberally dust the top of the pots with cocoa powder.

CANTUCCINI
& VIN SANTO

*Vin Santo is 'sainted wine'. It has its origins in the Catholic Church where
it was once given at mass with a cracker. It is made mostly in Tuscany from
indigenous Trebbiano and Malvasia grapes and is invariably very sweet.*

*It is occasionally served at the end of a meal as a digestive but much more
commonly it is offered with biscotti so that you can dunk your sweet biscuits
in the wine. I imagine that a good part of this little dessert's appeal is the ritual
involved and the religious undertones of receiving this naughty Eucharist.*

For 60 biscuits:
3 medium free-range egg whites
3 whole medium free-range eggs
400g caster sugar
Seeds from 2 vanilla pods
2 teaspoons sesame seeds
1 teaspoon fennel seeds
600g Italian 00 flour
4½ teaspoons baking powder
375ml sunflower oil
500g mixed walnuts, almonds and pistachios, roughly chopped
Excellent Vin Santo

Take a large mixing bowl and a wooden spoon and beat together
the egg whites, the whole eggs, the sugar and all the seeds – vanilla,
sesame and fennel. Make sure everything is nicely combined. Slowly add
the flour, the baking powder and the oil and continue to combine with
your spoon. Add the chopped nuts and mix thoroughly. Place, covered,
in the fridge and leave overnight to stiffen.

The next day, preheat the oven to 200°C/Gas 6. Oil a baking sheet and
line it with baking parchment. Lay the mixture in a mound like a long,
squat loaf of bread from one end of the tray to the other. You should be
able to fit two of these elongated mounds (about 30cm × 15cm × 4–5cm)
on the tray. Bake for 30 minutes in the preheated oven.

Remove from the oven and when cool enough to handle slice into 1cm
slices. Meanwhile, turn the oven down to 140°C/Gas 1. Lay the slices
flat on a wire rack and place back in the oven for 15–20 minutes, or until
the biscuits are completely dried out.

These cantuccini will last for weeks if stored in an airtight container.
To serve, place 2 biscuits alongside a chilled glass of Vin Santo.

WALNUT & HONEY SEMIFREDDO

Semifreddo, literally 'half-cold' in Italian, is a really lovely alternative to ice cream. This dessert was on the original menu at POLPO and was served in an ice cream cone rather than in a bowl. It is such a playful way to present the semifreddo and I suggest you do the same. You can get hold of all sorts of cones near the freezer section of your supermarket.

For four to six:
250g caster sugar
300g walnuts, roughly chopped
Vegetable oil
4 medium free-range eggs, separated
50ml Marsala
600ml whipping cream
Ice cream cones
Runny honey

Make the praline first by melting 200g of the caster sugar in a heavy-based pan with 2 tablespoons of water until it is the colour of terracotta. Quickly mix in the walnuts and pour onto an oiled tray. Leave to cool in the fridge. Once cooled, break into pieces, place in a food processor and whizz until it has the consistency of breadcrumbs.

Before starting to make the semifreddo, place a 1 litre metal container in the freezer. Now take 3 clean, cold mixing bowls. In the first bowl, use a hand-held electric whisk to whip the egg whites into stiff peaks and refrigerate. In the second bowl, whisk the egg yolks with the remaining 50g of sugar and the Marsala until pale and fluffy, then refrigerate. Lastly whisk the whipping cream to soft peaks.

Remove the first 2 bowls from the fridge and stir a large spoonful of the whipped egg whites into your egg yolk mixture until they are well combined and start to loosen it up. Now, one at a time, lightly fold a spoon of egg white and a spoon of whipped cream alternately into the yolk mixture, until everything is incorporated. With the last spoon add almost all the walnut praline, reserving a little for sprinkling over the finished semifreddo.

Place the semifreddo in your frozen metal container, cover in clingfilm, put back in the freezer and leave overnight. To serve, use an ice cream scoop to put a large ball of semifreddo into your cones. Dribble a little of the honey over the top and scatter the reserved crunchy praline.

CHOCOLATE SALAMI

*This isn't so much a dessert, but rather a small sweet taste to go with coffee,
like those enigmatically named petits fours. The fun here is had in the appearance
of the chocolate-and-nut sausage: it looks like salami. And when it is sliced,
it takes on the appearance of black pudding or blood sausage.*

4 medium free-range egg yolks
160g caster sugar
180g unsalted butter – at room temperature
100g cocoa powder
Good pinch of fine salt
200g mixed nuts – hazelnuts, walnuts, pistachios
150g dried fruit roughly chopped – one type or a mixture
    eg dried apricots, figs and prunes
200g Savoiardi sponge fingers, broken into 1cm pieces

Beat the egg yolks with the sugar, then add the butter, cocoa powder
and salt, beating all the while so that you create a creamy paste.

Mix in the nuts, fruit and broken biscuits and place the mixture on
a sheet of foil. Roll the mixture into a cylinder 5cm wide – like a large,
thick sausage. Wrap in greaseproof paper or clingfilm and refrigerate
overnight. Slice into rounds and serve with coffee.

GALANI CHERRY 'SANDWICH'

Venice during Carnevale is best avoided. The crowds are daunting and all that mask-wearing can be disconcerting. But there are some interesting sweets and biscuits that are made only at this time of the year that can take your mind off the madness, should you find yourself in Venice in February. Galani are sweet wafers, a bit like crunchy flat doughnuts. You could eat them on their own with liberal dustings of icing sugar or they are perfect for this boozy cherry 'sandwich'.

For six:
120g granulated sugar
250g pitted fresh cherries
30ml Kirsch
2 medium free-range eggs
50g caster sugar
2 tablespoons sunflower oil
50ml white wine
1 tablespoon rum
1 tablespoon grappa
250g Italian 00 flour
½ tablespoon baking powder
Pinch of fine salt
1 litre vegetable oil, for deep-frying
200ml whipping cream
Icing sugar, to serve

Mix the granulated sugar into 120ml water over a medium heat. Once the sugar has dissolved, turn up the heat and gently boil for a further 5 minutes. The sugar and water will have formed a gloopy syrup. Then add the pitted cherries and boil for 2 minutes more. Take off the heat and allow to cool. Stir in the Kirsch and set aside.

In a large bowl, beat the eggs and caster sugar with a whisk. Mix in the sunflower oil, white wine, rum and grappa. Slowly work in the flour and baking powder and a pinch of salt until you have a firm dough. Wrap the dough in clingfilm and leave it in the fridge to rest for 30 minutes.

Take the dough out and, using a pasta machine or rolling pin, create 12 paper-thin rectangles, 12cm × 6cm. These really do need to be as thin as you can possibly manage. Half fill a deep pan with the vegetable oil and bring it up to 190°C (or until a cube of bread dropped in the oil turns golden in less than a minute). Fry the slices of dough individually until golden brown and crisp. Drain on kitchen paper.

Whip the cream until it has soft peaks. To serve the sandwiches, spoon a small amount of the soft whipped cream onto your plates. On top of each place a galani wafer, some more whipped cream, a pile of cherries with their juices, another galani wafer and a good dusting of icing sugar.

ESSE BISCUITS

These little 'S'-shaped biscuits are traditionally made at Easter and are perfect for dunking in your milky coffee in the morning. They have a very subtle vanilla flavour with just the merest hint of lemon. Esse biscuits are particular to Venice but I have been unable to discover the significance of the letter S. The only explanation that has been offered is that Venice is known as La Serenissima — The Serene One, but this seems a little tenuous to me. If anyone has any clues, please let me know.

For twenty biscuits:
130g soft unsalted butter
120g caster sugar
250g Italian 00 flour
2 medium free-range egg yolks
2 teaspoons vanilla extract
Zest of 1 lemon
Pinch of fine salt
1–2 tablespoons cold milk

Place the butter and sugar in a food processor and whizz to combine into a soft paste. Add the flour, egg yolks, vanilla extract, lemon zest and salt. Add 1–2 tablespoons of milk gradually, adding the full amount (or more) if the mixture is too dry to be pliant.

Place the mixture on a floured work surface and bring together. Wrap it up in clingfilm and place in the fridge for 1 hour.

Preheat the oven to 170°C/Gas 3. Cut off pieces of the chilled dough and roll into cylinders, 15cm long and 2cm in diameter. Bend into S-shapes and put on a baking tray lined with baking parchment. Bake in the preheated oven for 10–15 minutes, or until only just golden.

Cool on a wire rack and store in an airtight container. They will keep for a good few days.

CIAMBELLA

There are so many different versions of this biscuity dessert that its name is almost meaningless. Order Ciambella in Lazio and you'll get a cake made from eggs, white wine and aniseed. Ask for the same thing in Calabria and a ring-shaped pudding made with boiled potatoes and flour will arrive. In Veneto, the dish is simpler than any of these versions and has the addition of chocolate sauce. It's still made in the distinctive ring shape and looks very impressive when taken to the table and sliced.

For twelve slices:

115g unsalted butter – at room temperature
220g caster sugar, plus more to sprinkle on top
450g Italian 00 flour
3 rounded teaspoons baking powder
Pinch of fine salt
2 medium free-range eggs
4 tablespoons milk
Finely grated zest of 1 lemon
350ml double cream
150g dark chocolate (at least 60% cocoa), grated

Preheat the oven to 200°C/Gas 6. Beat together the butter and 170g sugar in a large mixing bowl using an electric whisk until pale and creamy. Add the flour, baking powder, salt, eggs and milk and knead the dough until smooth. Work in the finely grated lemon zest.

On a baking tray lined with baking parchment, mould the dough into a large ring, like a fat tyre, leaving a gap of at least 5cm from the sides of the tray for the cake to spread. Sprinkle with more caster sugar and bake for 45 minutes.

To make the chocolate sauce, simply dissolve the remaining 50g sugar in 4 tablespoons of water in a heavy-based pan over a gentle heat and then turn up the heat and bring to the boil. Turn down to a simmer and keep stirring as the solution thickens and starts to caramelize, but be careful not to let it burn. Add the double cream and chocolate, bring slowly to the boil and stir until fully combined and glossy.

To serve, cut the Ciambella at the table and pour on the warm chocolate sauce.

WARM AUTUMN FRUITS WITH AMARETTO CREAM

This recipe takes three autumn fruits prepared in different ways and brings them together for a common cause. The pears are poached, the apples are caramelized and the figs are left to speak for themselves. When served, this dish looks incredibly simple but a little preparation is required. The pears can be any variety, but Comice are best. Use small round dessert apples. Make sure the figs are ripe; if they are not, you can cheat by roasting them before you use them. Quarter them, drizzle with a little honey and place on a baking tray for 15 minutes at 140°C/Gas 1.

For six:
500ml white wine
250g caster sugar – use vanilla sugar if you can
1 cinnamon stick, broken into two
3 firm pears
6 small dessert apples (3 if they are large)
A squeeze of lemon juice
200g unsalted butter
200g brown sugar
200g whipping cream
50ml Amaretto
6 ripe figs, quartered
4 Amaretti biscuits

Bring 1 litre of water, the wine, sugar and cinnamon stick to the boil in a medium-sized saucepan. Leave it bubbling for 5 minutes while you peel the pears, leaving the stalks intact. Pop the pears into the pot and simmer on a very low heat, covered, for approximately 1 hour, or until the pears are soft when pierced with a knife. Remove from the heat and allow to cool. When cool, cut the pears into quarters, removing the cores. Keep them in the syrup and discard the cinnamon stick.

Now peel, core and cut each apple in half if they are small, or into quarters if they are large. Keep in water with a good squeeze of lemon juice to stop them from going brown. In a wide pan melt the butter with the brown sugar. When this starts to boil add the apple pieces. Turn the temperature down and bubble on a low heat until tender (about 3–4 minutes). Remove from the heat and set aside. Finally, whisk the whipping cream to very soft peaks, then stir in the Amaretto.

Preheat the oven to 160°C/Gas 3. Take an ovenproof serving dish and spoon in the pears with some of their syrup, the apples with all their sauce and the quartered figs and place in the warm oven for 10 minutes. Remove from the oven, spoon over some of the cream and break the biscuits over the top. Place the whole dish in the middle of the table with a large serving spoon and six empty bowls.

FLOURLESS CHOCOLATE & HAZELNUT CAKE

Don't kid yourself that 'flourless' means 'calorie-free'. This lovely moist chocolate cake is packed with flavour and just so happens to be gluten-free. Although they are very different things, you still feel slightly virtuous. (It's that 'less' in the title, isn't it?)

The secret ingredient in this recipe is Frangelico, a terribly kitsch hazelnut liqueur that comes in a bottle shaped like a monk. It is very sweet and resonates powerfully of the 1970s. But don't let that put you off — it imparts an essential nutty hit to the overall flavour.

For twelve slices or more:
375g whole hazelnuts
375g chocolate (70% cocoa), melted
375g butter — at room temperature
200g soft brown sugar
175g caster sugar
9 medium free-range eggs
50ml Frangelico
2 tablespoons double cream
250g mascarpone

Preheat the oven to 180°C/Gas 4. Prepare a 26cm cake tin by greasing it with a little oil and lining with baking parchment.

Roast the hazelnuts in the oven for about 10 minutes, or until they are dark brown. Allow them to cool and then put them on the bottom half of a clean tea towel on a work surface. Fold over the other half of the tea towel and rub vigorously to remove the skins. Put the skinned nuts in a food processor and blitz until they have the consistency of breadcrumbs.

Melt the chocolate by placing it in a glass bowl and slowly heating the bowl over gently boiling water. Fold the hazelnuts through the chocolate. Put the butter and sugars in a bowl and use an electric whisk to make them pale and fluffy. Start adding the eggs two at a time, whilst whisking, alternating with spoonfuls of the chocolate and hazelnut mixture.

Scrape the whole mixture into your prepared tin and put into the preheated oven. Check the cake after 1 hour. The top of the cake should be set and a skewer put into the centre will come out still wet but not too raw (the cake settles down and sets inside as it cools). Whilst it is still warm, pierce the cake many times over the top with the skewer and sprinkle over the Frangelico. Allow the cake to cool completely in the tin.

Fold the double cream into the mascarpone until smooth. Cut the cake just before you want to eat it and serve with a generous spoonful of mascarpone cream.

PANNA COTTA WITH BLACKBERRIES

This is another dessert that works very well in its own separate pot. Just like the tiramisù on page 254, these little confections are made individually and are best in 150ml Duralex tumblers. Blackberries always taste better when you have picked them yourself, by the way.

For twelve or more:
750ml milk
800ml double cream
150g caster sugar
4 vanilla pods, split lengthways
20g leaf gelatine
25ml grappa
About 100 (500g) blackberries

In a heavy-based pan put the milk, double cream, 100g of the caster sugar and the seeds scraped out from the vanilla pods. Just before the liquid reaches boiling point, remove from the heat.

Soften the gelatine leaves in iced water for about 5 minutes. Squeeze out the water and stir into the creamy mixture along with the grappa.

Cool the liquid in a mixing bowl over ice, stirring occasionally to disperse the vanilla seeds. When it begins to set and the vanilla seeds are suspended in the mixture (this will take about an hour) transfer the setting liquid into a large jug. Pour into the twelve glasses, leave a 2cm gap at the top, and chill in the fridge until they are fully set. It is best to do this overnight.

Put the blackberries into a very large saucepan with 100ml water and the remaining 50g of caster sugar. On a very low heat, slowly poach the blackberries until they soften and start to lose their shape. Take off the heat and allow to cool slightly so that you can taste them. Add more sugar if you like.

When the blackberry compote has fully cooled, remove the 12 set panna cotta pots from the fridge and top each one with a generous spoonful or two. You can serve this with Cantuccini biscuits (see page 256).

SAFFRON PEARS WITH MERINGUE

The use of saffron in northern Italian cooking, notably in dishes such as Lombardy's Osso Buco con Risotto Milanese (see page 168), reminds us that the spice route passed straight through Venice for many centuries. Although it is most commonly used in savoury dishes, saffron here adds a subtle spice and hue to the pears. I also love the contrast in textures between the delicate flesh of the fruit and the crunch of the meringue, which in turn yields to a chew.

For six:
8 medium free-range egg whites – at room temperature
650g caster sugar
250ml white wine
6 firm pears – Comice are perfect
Pinch of saffron
200ml whipping cream

Preheat the oven to 130°C/Gas ½ and line 2 baking sheets with baking parchment paper. Tip the egg whites into a large clean mixing bowl (not plastic). Beat them with an electric hand-whisk on medium speed until the mixture resembles a fluffy cloud and stands up in stiff peaks when the blades are lifted.

Now turn the speed up and start to add 450g of the caster sugar, a little at a time. Continue beating for 3–4 seconds between each addition of sugar. It's important to add the sugar slowly at this stage as it helps prevent the meringue from weeping later. When ready, the mixture should be thick and glossy.

Stick down the edges of the paper with a little leftover mixture – this is to prevent the parchment lifting when baking. You can either dollop the meringue mixture into shallow 'nest' with a spoon or transfer your mixture to a piping bag and pipe down a thin base in a coil, working out from the centre and then up around the outside to build a more even, round 'nest'. Make 6 of these. Bake for about 1½ hours until the meringues sound crisp when tapped underneath. Remove from the oven and leave to cool.

Bring 1.5 litres of water, the wine and the remaining 200g sugar to the boil in a large saucepan. Turn the heat down to medium and leave the liquid bubbling while you peel the pears, remembering to leave the stalks intact. Put the pears into the saucepan with the pinch of saffron and simmer on a very low heat for approximately 1 hour or until the pears are soft when pierced with a knife. Remove from the heat and allow the pears to cool. Boil the liquid to reduce it to a thicker syrup. When the pears are cool, carefully remove the cores using a corer and quarter them. Keep them in the syrup and turn your attentions to the meringue.

Lightly whip the cream until it has a fluffy consistency. Now place a meringue onto each plate using a little whipped cream on the base to hold them in place. Dollop a large tablespoon of cream onto each meringue and then place the pears on top with a little of the syrup.

BLOOD ORANGE
& CAMPARI CAKE

Campari is one of the ingredients I most associate with Venice, even though it originates from Milan. Its bright red glow and sticky bitter taste are key elements of the quintessential Venetian drink, the Spritz. It's also the defining ingredient in a Negroni, and makes it a cocktail to be reckoned with.

My early trips to Venice found me in the Giardini neighbourhood at the end of the Grand Canal and I have a strong memory of the massive illuminated CAMPARI sign on top of the Hotel Riviera on Lido, now sadly gone.

Tom and I had always talked about creating a dessert that featured Campari and we asked one of our chefs, Florence Knight, to come up with some ideas. This was her winning response.

For twelve slices:
8 blood oranges
350g Greek yoghurt
600g caster sugar
4 medium free-range eggs, lightly beaten
250g butter, melted and cooled
350g fine semolina
100g ground almonds
100ml Campari

Preheat the oven to 170°C/Gas 3. Finely grate the zest of 4 of the oranges and set the fruit to one side. In a large mixing bowl put the yoghurt, 300g of the caster sugar and the lightly beaten eggs. Stir in the cooled butter and finally fold through all the dry ingredients including the orange zest. Scrape the mixture into a 23cm greased cake tin and put into the oven.

After 20 minutes, check to see if the cake is ready by gently pressing the centre to see if it springs back. Depending on your oven it may need a little more time. If it does, you can finally check by pushing a skewer into the middle; it should come out dry. Leave to cool in the tin.

While the cake is cooking, make the syrup. Put the juice of the 8 oranges, the remaining sugar and the Campari into a heavy-based saucepan. Slowly bring to the boil. Allow to simmer and skim off any white scum. When reduced to a medium-thick syrup remove from the heat.

Prick the top of the cake all over with a toothpick and spoon the syrup over the warm sponge in a couple of batches until everything has been absorbed. Your cake is now ready. To serve, simply cut a slice and offer with excellent vanilla ice cream.

DRINKS

As an amateur anthropologist I am interested in the subtle cultural indicators that distinguish people from different nations. Putting an unworn sweater on your shoulders with the arms folded loosely in front of your neck is a particularly Italian trait, not something one would expect from a Scot or a Turk. Italian men often like to wear brightly coloured spectacle frames; you will rarely see an Englishman in anything other than sober steel or dark plastic. To show your appreciation of good food in a bar in Verona, you might throw your used paper napkin onto the floor. In London, a similar act in a pub would be seen as rude and loutish.

The differences in drinking culture are noteworthy, too. It is quite common to sip a glass of wine or beer at 11am in Italy. Such alcoholic enthusiasm would be frowned upon in Britain. In the US it would be positively shocking. But it is the type of drink that each of these cultures favours that is most striking. In the UK, the national pre-meal tipple is probably the gin and tonic. In New York you'd have a Martini. In northern Italy, and in Venice particularly, it is the Spritz.

Spritz is nearly always made with the local white wine. As you eat and drink your way around the city, you will notice that wine is often served in tiny glasses. These allow you to have just a small taste before you move on to the next bàcaro. The wines served are almost all young, local varieties too: Garganega from Veneto, Pinot Bianco from Friuli, Barbera from Piedmont. Even on formal occasions there is rarely any ceremony with wine, no pretentious flourishes, no showing off: the wine is often poured from barrel or bottle straight into a decorated clay jug and then into small glasses or tumblers.

I strongly recommend you try this at home too. It gives the wine a lower status than perhaps you are used to if you dine in tableclothed restaurants, but I feel that this is right with humble food shared amongst friends. There is also something tactile and homely about a small peasant glass that you don't get with an expensive balloon.

What wine should you drink with the recipes in this book? Stick to the varieties mentioned above and from the northern regions of Veneto, Alto Adige, Lombardy, Emilia Romagna, Piedmont and Friuli-Venezia Giulia. It's what we do at POLPO and it seems to work rather well.

SPRITZ

A Spritz is a mixture of white wine (sometimes sparkling Prosecco is used), a bitter such as Campari or Aperol and a splash of soda water. The garnish should always be a slice of lemon and sometimes an olive too. Of course, there are many ways to make this drink and you will always find someone with a strong opinion telling you that it must be made this way or it should only ever be made like that... Well, this is how we make ours.

The only choice you need to make is Campari or Aperol. The former has a sharp, bitter quality and gives the drink more of a punch. The latter is slightly sweeter, still with an underlying bitterness, but is milder too with only 11 per cent alcohol compared to 25 per cent. Campari was invented in 1860 by Gaspare Campari and to this day, the exact recipe remains a closely guarded secret. The distinctive red hue comes from the original addition of crushed cochineal insects. Aperol is flavoured with gentian flowers, orange bitters, rhubarb and cinchona bark and was developed by the Barbieri family of Padua in 1919.

For one:
Ice
1 large green olive, drained of brine
75ml white wine – something simple from Veneto like
    a Garganega or a Pinot Bianco
50ml either Campari or Aperol
Splash of soda water
1 slice of lemon

Take a large tumbler and fill it with ice. Push a large green olive (not one that has been kept in oil) onto the end of a cocktail skewer and pop it in the bottom of the glass. Pour the wine. Pour the Campari or Aperol. Add a short squirt of soda water and then a slice of lemon.

AMERICANO

*This is a refreshing seltzer invented by Mr Campari for his Caffè Campari.
It was originally called Milano-Torino because of the origins of the two main
ingredients, but later became known as the Americano after Gaspare noticed
many Americans enjoying the drink. It is favoured on more than one occasion
by Ian Fleming's James Bond. He orders one in the short story 'A View to a
Kill' and says of it: 'In cafés you have to drink the least offensive of the musical
comedy drinks.' It is delightfully inoffensive but still has that characteristic
bitterness so essential in Italian aperitifs.*

For one:
Ice
30ml sweet vermouth
30ml Campari
Soda water
Orange slice

Use a large tumbler filled with ice and pour the vermouth and the
Campari over the rocks. Top up with soda. Add the orange slice.
Like all seltzers, sip this one slowly and enjoy it as a long drink.

NEGRONI

What a brilliant concoction this is. There is such symmetry and balance here that it can't fail to bring a smile to your face or a spring to your step. The drink was invented, legend has it, when Count Camillo Negroni asked a bartender to add a slug of gin instead of soda to his Americano.

Orson Welles had a thing about Negronis and claimed that they were good for you. He maintained that while the gin might not be great for your liver, the bitters were, and the two balanced each other out. Try telling that to your doctor.

For one:
Ice
25ml gin
25ml Campari
25ml sweet vermouth
A slice of orange

Don't mess with these proportions. They are perfect as they are.

Fill a small tumbler with ice. Pour the ingredients over the ice, stir once or twice and add a slice of orange.

NEGRONI SBAGLIATO

The tale attached to this cocktail is almost as tasty as the drink itself. The story goes that a clumsy bartender grabbed a bottle of Prosecco instead of gin when fixing a Negroni and the resulting mistake ('sbagliato' means 'wrong') was preferred by the punter. It seems all Italian cocktails have been created accidentally by bartenders making mistakes or difficult customers wanting to change classic recipes. And thank goodness.

For one:
Ice
25ml sweet vermouth
25ml Campari
25ml Prosecco
Orange slice

Fill a tall glass with ice. Pour over the vermouth and Campari. Carefully top up with Prosecco. Add the orange slice and stir once.

BELLINI

Probably invented in Harry's Bar in Venice and named in honour of the fifteenth-century Venetian artist. It is important to use fresh white peach purée for this drink. It will not be the same with peach juice or, heaven forbid, peach liqueur. Just don't. Thankfully, white peach purée is available in good supermarkets and food halls.

For one:
25ml chilled white peach purée
100ml chilled Prosecco

Use a small straight glass rather than a champagne flute; it's much more authentic and a lot less naff. Pour the peach purée into the bottom of the glass, then top up with Prosecco. Using a long handled bar spoon, gently stir the mixture.

ELDERFLOWER
LEMONADE

Here's a refreshing cocktail, perfect for a spring or summer's day, light and floral and non-alcoholic, and one of the most popular drinks at POLPO. It's what we offer to children (and designated drivers) if all the grown-ups are drinking Bellinis.

For one:
Ice
25ml lemon juice
15ml elderflower cordial
Ginger beer to top up
Fresh mint, to serve

Put a handful of ice into a cocktail shaker and add the lemon juice and the elderflower cordial. Shake vigorously for 10 seconds and then pour the entire contents, ice too, into a highball glass. The mixture will have become very frothy. Top up with ginger beer and add a sprig of mint and a straw.

MOCK CLOVER CLUB

The real Clover Club is a gin-based cocktail that dates from the start of the twentieth century. It was created at the club of the same name in Philadelphia and enjoyed massive popularity before Prohibition put an end to all the fun.

This version removes the alcohol but retains the fun and is like a grown-up version of that popular American kid's cocktail, the Shirley Temple.

For one:
5ml free-range egg white
15ml lemon juice
15ml grenadine
55ml cranberry juice
Ice
1 maraschino cherry

In a Boston glass or a large jug whisk the egg white until slightly foamy. Add the lemon juice, grenadine and cranberry juice and fill with ice. Shake hard and strain into a fancy glass. Garnish with a single maraschino cherry.

GAZETTEER

A short and subjective
guide to some of Venice's
wine bars and restaurants

It is fair to say that Venice is an unforgettable city. If you have been before, you will have many vivid memories and fond recollections. But I am going to ask you to put those aside and try to forget them. In order to appreciate the living and breathing city (as opposed to the theme park tourist destination) you have to recalibrate your expectations and start from scratch. You need to see Venice with fresh eyes and from a less elevated angle. You need to approach it through the staff entrance, not through the elaborately gilded Gothic lobby and certainly not through the gift shop.

The clearest contrast between these two versions of Venice is to be found in the two squares of St Mark's and St Margherita.

I have an uneasy relationship with St Mark's Square. Often described as Europe's drawing room, frequently to be found on lists of favourite tourist attractions, incessantly photographed, full of pigeons, flanked by rip-off tea shops, overcrowded, getting ever-fuller with vile trinket stands selling plastic gondolas and carnival masks... do you see where this is going yet? Yes, I'm afraid I have visited Venice often enough to have realized that you only have to see St Mark's Square three times, and then you must never go back again.

The first visit will leave your mouth hanging open as you wonder at the majesty of the square, the beautiful architecture, the crumbling basilica and the campanile pointing skywards like a giant finger that seems to be saying, 'Hey, God, have you seen *this*?' Then there is the Doge's Palace with its fortress-like façade, hiding goodness knows how many dark secrets, the two columns that face the lagoon holding aloft two clumsy statues, one of the winged lion of St Mark and the other of what looks like St George with a slain dragon, but is actually St Theodore with a limp crocodile. Take it all in. Marvel at it. Visit the attractions if you have to. Get it out of your system.

Your second visit should be at night when the city has gone to sleep. The square takes on a tranquil serenity. It seems to be saying 'Ah, peace at last!' The regiments of low-wattage streetlamps make an impossibly pretty scene. I once visited at night during 'acqua alta', a period of high tide that afflicts the city from time to time. St Mark's Square was flooded and the buildings and lights were reflected perfectly in the water that covered the square like a shallow lake.

Your third visit will be horrible. You will notice the heaving crowds, the tourist tat, the slavish video camera filming, the noise, the pigeons, the pigeon droppings... You should immediately exit the square to the west, by the Museo Correr, follow the signs to Accademia, cross the bridge, hang right at the Accademia gallery, cross the first bridge on Rio San Trovaso, cross Campo San Barnaba, take a right over the Ponte dei Pugni (Bridge of Fists) and enter Campo Santa Margherita.

If St Mark's Square is the big Hollywood blockbuster that breaks box-office records, then Campo Santa Margherita is the classy independent movie that wins all the Oscars. It is a slice of real Venice and I love it. Here you will find genuine Venetians: teachers from the nearby university, artists, students, poets, politicians, bohemians and musicians.

Once you have taken ten or twenty minutes to wander around the campo to familiarize yourself with your new favourite place, you should head straight to the Red Caffè in the middle of the square to the west and treat yourself to a drink. You must be thirsty. You deserve it. And if it is anytime after 11am then that drink might be a Spritz.

Campo Santa Margherita is, unlike St Mark's, a living square. Over to the south you will see a clumsy cube of a building dropped incongruously onto the campo at an angle. It's part of the old scuola and is used mostly now as a place to paint goalposts so that the local scamps can play football. Very important. But it also displays an ancient stone tablet into which are carved the minimum permitted size of fish, a reminder that the famously bureaucratic northern Italians were exactly the same centuries ago. There is a similar tablet at the fish market in Rialto. The fishmongers of Campo Santa Margherita still sell their wares close to this tablet, as they must have done for several hundred years. You have got to admire that respect for tradition. Most days there are three fishmongers who set up shop, preferring this boutique positioning rather than the outré Rialto pitch.

There may not be the permanently buzzing atmosphere that you get in the daddy of all fish markets but the fish here is of the same exceptional quality and it's much more convenient to the many locals than the forty-minute round trip to that other place. They don't even seem to mind when the occasional stray football knocks against their Wellington-booted shins. (The pigeons around here eat the tossed-away offcuts, you will notice. Now that is classy. You won't find St Mark's Square pigeons dining on sashimi.)

In the centre of the square are two wells, a reminder that this was once the field where the villagers of this district would come for water. There might have been a few cows, too. The wells are probably still functioning today; there are certainly plenty of freshwater taps around Venice, always on, including one here in the square. Go on – take a drink. The water is fine.

Unusually for Venice there are mature sycamores in the campo here providing shade in the harsh summer months and relief all year round for dogs. They also house hundreds of the most exquisitely tiny sparrows who are so bold that they will land on the table, right in front of you, and eat crisps from your hand. It's massively charming but I am told that the salt is very bad for them.

As you look around the square you will see other stalls and tradespeople. There's usually a greengrocer here towards the north (that's your left as you sit outside the Red Caffè) but the local star is the floating grocer to the south, out of the square towards Campo San Barnaba.

His shop is a barge on the canal under the Ponte dei Pugni. This bridge is where bare-knuckle fights would take place according to certain rules. You can see the polished marble feet showing where the fighters would have stood on top of the bridge.

But what of the rest of the food in the square? Unfortunately, it's not great. The menus at the three or four restaurants that extend way into the middle of the immense centre read more like compendia of every popular Italian dish ever invented rather than a considered expression of local seasonal ingredients. Best to get a fantastic over-filled tramezzino in the Red Caffè behind you. And another Spritz.

It is possible to eat very well at many places in Venice, often without even sitting down. The locals do what they describe as a giro di ombre – a sort of preprandial pub crawl where one takes a cichèto and a glass of wine in each bàcaro before moving on to the next. On the following pages are twelve places that I am particularly fond of. Some are bàcari, some are restaurants. All are essential Venetian experiences.

CAMPO SANTA MARGHERITA; CAMPO SAN BARNABA (BELOW)

1 THE RED CAFFÈ
2 CANTINONE GIÀ SCHIAVI
3 NICO
4 ALLE TESTIERE
5 CORTE SCONTA
6 I RUSTEGHI
7 ALLA VEDOVA
8 LA CANTINA
9 PARADISO PERDUTO
10 ALL'ARCO
11 DO MORI
12 AL MERCÀ

THE RED CAFFÈ

Dorsoduro 2963, Campo Santa Margherita – Vaporetto Ca' Rezzonico
Telephone: (+39) 041 528 7998

It was at the Red Caffè (I have heard it called Caffè Rosso – it is
painted red) that I realized the signature aperitif at POLPO needed to
be a Spritz. We still use exactly the same recipe that they use at this tiny
Venetian student bar. You could stand inside the bar with the huge brass
and copper Elektra coffee machine looking like a rocket ship from a Jules
Verne story, the impossibly thick tramezzini sandwiches filled to within
an inch of their lives with egg and tinned tuna and the cool tattooed kids
on both sides of the bar, or you could pay a few cents extra and sit outside.
Here, at your table, with your Spritz in hand, you can survey the greatest
single slice of Venetian life you will get in one sitting. Forget St Mark's
Square, for all life is here.

CANTINONE GIÀ SCHIAVI

Dorsoduro 992, Ponte San Trovaso – Vaporetto Accademia
Telephone: (+39) 041 523 0034

If you stay in the Dorsoduro district of Venice then you will come across
the Cantinone già Schiavi on several occasions as you criss-cross the
side canals and wander through the charming alleyways behind the
Accademia gallery. It is on a particularly pretty canal, diagonally opposite
one of the last remaining and most famous gondola repair yards in Venice.

From the outside, the Cantinone looks like a wine shop. When you
are inside, it still looks like a wine shop. Actually, it *is* a wine shop but
it has a small crisis of identity in that it also happens to be one of the most
characterful bàcari in all of Venice.

The place gets very busy in mid- to high-season from noon till early
evening, and quite often the crowds spill out onto the San Trovaso bridge
and along the sides of the canal. What are they all coming for? Well, in
part for the excellent selections of wines, grappa and Italian specialist
bitters by the bottle. Partly, also, for the great range of local wines
available by the glass at the battered marble bar. There are usually ten or
twelve on offer. But mostly they come for Alessandra's fabled cichèti.

Alessandra, or Sandra as she likes to be known, is the typical Italian
matriarch. There are her four strapping sons, serious-looking, economical
in conversation, tending the bar. The men seem to get on with their work

in a detached, slightly world-weary way. Sandra, however, works at the other end of the bar nearest the window that looks out onto the canal. She labours with a cheery industriousness: almost as fast as she can cut the bread, trim the mortadella and spread the baccalà, it is all going out, cichèto after cichèto, crostino after crostino, plate after plate. She will occasionally ask a small group to stand away from her work counter so that the crowds behind can push through to place their order. I estimate that she serves 100 to 120 people an hour in busy periods. I am sure on some days she will feed as many as 600 people.

One morning she let me come early to watch her preparing the cichèti for the day's onslaught. By 9am when I arrived, she had already laid out much of the day's offer in the large glass cabinet that she works behind. I know from many visits that she continues to prepare, replenish and serve all the way through to early evening, or until the food runs out, whichever is sooner.

NICO

Dorsoduro 922, Fondamenta Zattere al Ponte Longo – Vaporetto Zattere
Telephone: (+39) 041 522 5293

Nico is a something of an institution and enjoys one of the prettiest spots in Venice, overlooking the beautiful island of Giudecca and its wide canal. It faces south, too, and gets bathed in sunshine for virtually the whole day for most of the year. How appropriate, then, that it sells ice cream.

There is a slight schizophrenia to its personality, however. Inside, it evokes the formica and polished steel era of the fifties and sixties. There is a television showing football and bright strip lighting hanging over the long high bar and scattered café tables. Outside, the operation is totally geared up for the thousands of tourists who descend on Venice as day-trippers from the appalling ocean liners that slice through the Giudecca Canal.

But locals and tourists come here for the same reason – the very good ice cream. There is little food that is worth mentioning apart from this but they do make a decent Spritz using Select, an esoteric Italian bitter.

From top left clockwise: THE RED CAFFÈ;
CANTINONE GIÀ SCHIAVI; NICO; THE RED CAFFÈ

ALLE TESTIERE

Castello 5801, Calle del Mondo Novo – Vaporetto Rialto
Telephone: (+39) 041 522 7220

Alle Testiere is an osteria, in other words, a hostelry. Not too far away, there are places bordering St Mark's Square and others in the shadow of Rialto Bridge that will haughtily call themselves 'ristorante'. No lofty nomenclature for this little place, though. The humble labelling belies a noble and honourable purpose. Alle Testiere almost accidentally offers the best food to be found in the whole city. And they do this by sticking to their hard and fast philosophy of opening the restaurant only on market days and writing the menu only when they have seen what's available at market that morning. It gets better. Then they prepare what they have bought in the most sympathetic way possible. You will never find a heavy sauce here or a baked pasta dish, or pizza (heaven forbid) or even Lombardian or Sicilian dishes. No. What you get here is that unwritten rule writ large: keep it simple.

The owners Bruno and Luca are quietly, almost shyly passionate about product, provenance, authenticity and simplicity. They are proud of their city and of its natural resources. Their menu never strays from having a total respect for the raw materials of the constituent ingredients. You would be hard pressed to find a more honest aesthetic in a restaurant anywhere in the world than here at Alle Testiere.

The way that the restaurant is interwoven with their lives is also worth mentioning. Alle Testiere is closed all of August and for a long period over Christmas and New Year. Everyone that works there gets a guaranteed seven-week break a year. In addition, the restaurant closes for two days every week ensuring that everyone gets weekly rest. The staff go on fishing trips together, harvest mussels together, visit winemakers together and seem to inhabit the restaurant just as the restaurant inhabits them. The novelist Donna Leon, a customer of Alle Testiere, says, 'Luca and Bruno have managed to capture the culinary heart of the city.'

CORTE SCONTA

Castello 3886, Calle del Pestrin – Vaporetto Arsenale
Telephone: (+39) 041 522 7024

Corte Sconta, which means 'hidden courtyard', has for many years been wowing Venetians, international gourmands and the crowds that flock yearly to the Venice film festival in nearby Giardini. It delivers world-class cooking in a sophisticated but relaxed setting and makes it all look so easy. Of course it isn't. The skill with which the owner Rita orchestrates the kitchen and front-of-house teams is impressive, especially because she makes it seem like she isn't even trying.

Rita is always immaculately dressed in timelessly elegant clothes. Her copper-red hair means that she is visible in the room no matter where you are seated and she manages to get to every table at least once during your meal to chat about the food, your visit and to make sure you are having a wonderful time. You usually are.

I always used to look forward to one dish in particular: John Dory fillets with orange and pink peppercorns. This dish was created by Rita's late husband and appears on page 131 in his honour.

I RUSTEGHI

San Marco 5513, Campiello del Tentor – Vaporetto Rialto
Telephone: (+39) 041 523 2205

Giovanni, the proudly Venetian owner of this well-hidden wine bar, is rather famous in the city for his imposing physique and forthright opinions. He presides over his baby with passion and care, although he can sometimes be slightly scary – I have seen him brood and glower if people show a lack of respect for his wines, his wares or his ways. In a good mood, however, he can be the most knowledgeable, entertaining and convivial host in Venice.

I Rusteghi is particularly difficult to find. It may only be one hundred steps from Rialto Bridge but you have to make sure they are exactly the right one hundred steps. Once you are off the bridge and onto Campo San Bartolomio, it's second right, first left, bear left, bear right, turn left, then turn right into the sottoportego. Got that? (My advice is to consult a map beforehand so that you know where you're going.)

The bar is in a beautiful courtyard where you can hear a pin drop, despite its proximity to one of the busiest tourist destinations in the world. Miraculous.

Ask Giovanni for his recommendations for delicious local wines and be sure to try some of the excellent cured meats, sliced wafer-thin on a gigantic red, hand-cranked machine.

From top left clockwise: ALLE TESTIERE;
ALLE TESTIERE; I RUSTEGHI; I RUSTEGHI

ALLA VEDOVA

Cannaregio 3912, Ramo Ca' d'Oro — Vaporetto Ca' d'Oro
Telephone: (+39) 041 528 5324

This is probably the most famous of all the bàcari and osterie in Venice and with good reason. It is evocative, atmospheric and won't have changed much in the last hundred years or so. It is colloquially known as Alla Vedova — the widow's place — although its official name is Ca' d'Oro.

The proprietor is Mirella who quietly oversees the whole operation. In the evening the tables are always full, booked in advance by those coming to sample the famous Dalmatian scampi dish Spaghetti alla Busara. But those in the know come during the day and stand at the tiny bar with a few cichèti — in particular the meatballs.

The meatballs — or polpette in Italian — are especially deserving of mention. They are soft spheres of ground veal, seasoned with white pepper and coated in breadcrumbs before being fried. They are rightly famous and alone worth the pilgrimage.

Other great snacks at this handsome pit stop include a delicious warm octopus salad and an impressive array of grilled vegetables displayed in large white serving dishes in a glass cabinet. I am very fond of the painted terracotta jugs that are used to pour the small selection of local wines.

LA CANTINA

Cannaregio 3689, Campo San Felice — Vaporetto Ca' d'Oro
Telephone: (+39) 041 522 8258

One of my favourite Venetian eccentrics is Francesco Zorzetto, co-owner of La Cantina just off Strada Nova. He is a passionate exponent of simple food prepared with the finest ingredients and the greatest care. Here is how you find him...

After a morning of exploring the fruit and vegetable market at Rialto you will probably need your second coffee of the day at Caffè del Doge on Calle dei Cinque. Then you will want to explore the fish market, marvelling at the local varieties of eel and grouper, crab and octopus. When it gets to about 11am, you should head to the little wooden jetty at the edge of the fish market where it meets the Grand Canal. This is the landing place for the traghetto, a beat-up, decommissioned gondola that ferries market-goers from one side of the canal to the other. The fare is a few coins. So you take the traghetto to the other side, making sure you observe the local etiquette: ladies may sit, gentlemen should not; it is considered un-manly. Once off the boat, walk a few steps and turn left onto Strada Nova and then, after a few minutes' walk, you will come to La Cantina on the left-hand side.

La Cantina is one of a small number of new bàcari where there is an emphasis on simple food, excellent local wines and friendly, knowledgeable service. What you also get here is the personality of the owners, Francesco and Andrea. Tom Oldroyd, our head chef, spent a week in Venice researching dishes and fell into conversation with Francesco who invited Tom to spend some time in the kitchen with him. Francesco's methods are meticulous. As you watch him work, you can see concentration etched on his face as he carves each piece of prosciutto di Parma on the immense Berkel slicer. His passion also manifests itself in other ways; Tom saw him throw a knife into a wall with a terrifying thud.

He is massively generous and good-natured, loves to spoil people with wines they may not have tried and he can be theatrically flamboyant too; I have watched him slice open a bottle of Prosecco with a sabre.

PARADISO PERDUTO

Cannaregio 2540, Fondamenta della Misericordia – Vaporetto San Marcuola
Telephone: (+39) 041 720 581

As you wander north from Strada Nova towards the Ghetto, the original Jewish quarter, the tourists get thinner on the ground and the city takes on a quieter air. There is a sort of grid system to the canals and Venice feels less cluttered and more open.

But there is a bàcaro here that is so raucous and lively that you would think you were in the city centre. Paradiso Perduto is a large room by Venetian standards, has a fantastically stocked bar and a counter groaning under the weight of delicious cichèti. The long rows of tables are laid out canteen-style so that you rub shoulders with strangers who will always end the evening as your new best friends.

There are steaming plates of spaghetti with local clams and a particularly good Bìgoli in Salsa (pasta with anchovies). The house seems to specialize in crustacea, such is their abundance in the displays at the large bar, and I particularly like the emphasis on unusual wines, such as the slightly frothy Prosecco col fondo (Prosecco aged on its lees).

It is a warm and welcoming place that is filled with consistently and genuinely interesting people – artists, students, bohemians and hippies. Although it is a little further from the centre, it is worth the schlep.

From top left clockwise: LA CANTINA;
LA CANTINA; ALLA VEDOVA;
LA CANTINA; PARADISO PERDUTO

ALL'ARCO

San Polo 436, Calle dell'Occhialer – Vaporetto Rialto Mercato
Telephone: (+39) 041 520 5666

This miniature bàcaro pulls off an astonishing feat: in a space no bigger than the average suburban sitting room it delivers some of the best food to be found anywhere in the city.

It is a bàcaro in the truest sense – standing room only, point and eat, simple local wines by the glass and an eclectic social melting pot of politicians, lecturers, market traders, in-the-know tourists and gourmands.

The place is run by father-and-son team Francesco and Matteo Pinto and its proximity to the fish market is one of the reasons the cichèti on offer are so startlingly fresh. All'Arco is the place to come for the best Baccalà Mantecato (creamed salt cod) and if you ask nicely, Francesco will conjure up an impromptu Bìgoli in Salsa (pasta with anchovies) in his 'kitchen' – a corner of the bar with a sink and a single hob.

On a Saturday Venice floods with tourists from the mainland, Italian day-trippers who the locals refer to quaintly as 'forèsti', and this wine bar is clearly on their radar; it gets packed. Not difficult, you may think, considering its size, but when you see the crowds spill into the calle outside in their hundreds you realize that this place has a reputation.

As with many of these small bars run by passionate people, the best time to go to All'Arco is off-peak, around midday or late afternoon, and get into conversation. Before you know it Francesco or Matteo will be asking you to try something they are particularly proud of. It's a tiny slice of real culinary Venice.

DO MORI

San Polo 429, Calle dei Do Mori – Vaporetto Rialto Mercato
Telephone: (+39) 041 522 5401

Just across the alleyway from All'Arco is the oldest bàcaro in all of Venice. Reportedly established in 1462, Do Mori seems to have changed very little in five and a half centuries. It is named after the two Moors who once manned the barrels full of Custoza from the vineyards of Lake Garda and Merlot from the foothills of the Dolomites. It really is nothing more than a dark corridor between two narrow calle with a bar to one side and beaten copper cauldrons hanging from the ceiling. But it is so compellingly atmospheric that it is an essential stop on any tour of Venice's watering holes.

The food on offer here is basic and in the category of 'convenient' rather than epicurean but what Do Mori does, it does well. The tramezzini are worth noting because of their dinky proportions: they are cut into small squares rather than the traditional triangles and are known affectionately as 'francobolli' – postage stamps. The usual suspects of Sardèle in Saór (sardines in vinegar) and Baccalà Mantecato (creamed salt cod) are present and correct and in winter you might be lucky enough to find steaming cotechino in a soup tureen behind the counter.

The early-rising keepers of this little place are short on charm but tend to get more animated when the market traders come in for their first glass of wine shortly after 10am. You will notice that there are two distinct crowds here: the locals who hover near the entrance closest to the market and tourists who gather at the doors that lead to Calle dei Do Mori. I like to stand right in the middle where the food is.

AL MERCÀ

San Polo 213, Campo Bella Vienna – Vaporetto Rialto Mercato
No telephone

It is easy to find this place simply by looking for the largest crowd on the periphery of the fruit and vegetable market at Rialto. The wine bar itself is tiny with barely enough room behind it to pour an ombra, let alone swing a cat. So tight is space, in fact, that in order to get behind the counter to work, the bartender must push the cash register into the space and shimmy sideways before sliding the till back. It is as comical as it sounds. But the massive crowds of students, professionals and tourists spill outwards onto the campo in front of Al Mercà and are testament to the charm and appeal of this famous pit stop and meeting place.

What to drink? A Spritz, of course. Made here in tall, stemmed wine glasses and glowing red or orange, you will see one in everyone's hand as they stand and gossip or argue about local politics. The food is limited but surprisingly good and very distinctive – Al Mercà specializes in little crusty panini made with good bread and serious ingredients. The fact that it is located next to the most famous cheese shop in Venice (Casa del Parmigiano) must come in very handy.

From top left clockwise: ALL' ARCO;
ALL' ARCO; AL MERCÀ; ALL' ARCO;
DO MORI

ACKNOWLEDGEMENTS

Firstly, I am indebted to Tom Oldroyd, who turned my vague notes and notions at our first meetings into real three-dimensional dishes, and who gave form and flesh to the POLPO menu. Tom reinterpreted traditional Venetian recipes so that we could offer them as small plates to a London audience, while contributing fresh takes on familiar dishes. His cooking is always intelligent, simple and delicious. I also want to thank Tom for his invaluable assistance in getting the nitty-gritty of the recipes down on paper.

Tom and I would also like to thank Mattia Antionini, Florence Knight and Rachel O'Sullivan, who have assisted so well with the menus and in the various kitchens of our little family of restaurants. Tom's personal thanks go to Juliet Peston and Sue Lewis for their guidance, wisdom and talent.

Profound gratitude and respect to my business partner and friend Richard Beatty, who has valiantly put up with my tantrums and wailings since we first decided to open a restaurant. We have an agreement that we will carry on doing this as long as we laugh more than we cry.

A big thank you to Luke Bishop and all the staff past and present who have worked so hard for the success of POLPO and its siblings. It is the day-in, day-out dedication of our staff that has been the engine of our restaurants. Chefs, porters, bartenders, waiters, hosts, managers and supervisors: thank you all.

I must heartily thank Richard Atkinson at Bloomsbury for his patient, meticulous editing. Thank goodness, too, for the significant nous of his colleagues Natalie Hunt and Hattie Ellis. Mille grazie. And I'm indebted to Jenny Zarins for taking such gorgeous photographs and for capturing the breathtaking beauty of Venice.

Thanks to David Tanguy for designing such an exquisite book and also to those who have brilliantly assisted in various creative endeavours along the way: Georgie Clarke, Tabitha Hawkins, Guglielmo Rossi, Xa Shaw Stewart and Bruce McNally.

Thank you to Eugenie Furniss and Cathryn Summerhayes at William Morris for starting, and keeping, the ball rolling, and to POLPO's publicist Tanya Layzell-Payne, for convincing me that writing a book would be a good idea.

And finally, I would like to thank my wife Jules for her patience, advice and encouragement. It is only because of her support that I have been able to realize my modest achievements. I dedicate this book to her, to our daughters Martha and Mabel, and to our son Ollie.

Canale che va a Mestre

RAILY TO PADUA TREVISO &c

Ponte della Laguna

Railway
Station
Staziona della Strada Ferrata

Isola S. Chiara

CANAL GRANDE

Campo di Marti

CANALE DI FERRO GRANDE

Ponte di Ferro GRAND

Riva delle Zattere

CANALE CHE VA A FUSINA

CANALE DELLA GIU